Out of the Whirlwind

The Major Message of

Job

L. D. Johnson

Broadman Press
Nashville, Tennessee

© Copyright 1971 ● Broadman Press
All rights reserved
ISBN: 0-8054-1208-5
4212-08

Scripture quotations are from the Revised
Standard Version unless otherwise indicated

Library of Congress Catalog Card Number: 78-145983
Dewey Decimal Classification: 223.1
Printed in the United States of America
6.S7017

Contents

To Marion

Foreword—

Unlike almost any other biblical character, Job is Everyman, except that both his virtue and his suffering are far beyond ours. Yet, despite familiarity with Job, one has the feeling that his secret is not widely known. People tend to think of him only superficially as "patient Job" who stood steadfast under the blows of an incredible misfortune and, as a reward, received double for all he had lost. There is only enough truth in that understanding to conceal the real message. Another book about Job may not be needed, but I welcome the opportunity to share what I believe to be its inner and deeper meanings. This is more an affirmation of faith than an abbreviated and hasty attempt at scholarship. I have listened to and read others who are learned and wise, and tried to profit from their insights. Much is owed to one's teachers. But in the last analysis what I know of Job comes out of my heart. At least it has come through it.

For a long time Job has been an object of fascination. During the past eight years he has been a special kind of companion. I have wept and railed with him, alternated with him between despair and defiance, felt his outrage and his wonder, asked his questions and affirmed his hope and confidence. I have admired his integrity and courage and wished for such credits. And at the depths I have found that Job's experience is not unlike our own—God speaks from the whirlwind.

Trying to set down what I see in Job is a task attempted numerous times over recent years. But the bottom has never been reached, for like a well springing up, its resources seem exhaustless. Every time the bucket goes down it comes up with a fresh supply. If I know myself this won't be my final word on Job, but it is a considered one.

Nor will my efforts satisfy everyone. To some the interpretations will appear too traditional; to others they will sound strange. And because they are different from the interpretations of some, to such they will doubtless be suspect, perhaps even threatening. I would consider it arrogantly immature to try to be different for the sake of doing so, or to declare as demonstrated fact what is only personal opinion. But I will not write about the Bible with an eye on some imagined outraged fellow-believer who disagrees with what I write. Almost least of all would I do that about Job. Instead, I long for the day when honest and believing men can seek, without mutual suspicion and recrimination, to witness to each other concerning what they understand the Holy Spirit to be saying to them through the Scriptures.

The thesis of my interpretation of the book of Job is neither original nor complex. It is that the author of Job is dealing with the basic issue as to whether or not man ought to serve God without the expectation of being rewarded for doing so. Job's answer is a resounding affirmation. Although that is primary, there are other important issues in the book. I have attempted to treat these as adequately as the limitations allowed. I have thought that I could best help the reader by first introducing the book of Job, then giving an expository birds-eye view of its contents, and concluding with a look at some of the timeless questions raised by the author of Job.

I am grateful to Broadman Press for believing that what I have to say about Job would add something to the significance of the special annual Bible study of my denomination. If it does I shall be pleased.

L. D. JOHNSON

PART I
An Introduction to the Book of Job

CHAPTER 1
Job: The Book for Everyman

Anyone who ever wonders if we get what is coming to us in this life needs to read the book of Job. Is life a surefire deal, neatly packaged and delivered on the doorstep—so much for so much? Are wrong choices always punished and right ones always rewarded, like the rat in the researcher's laboratory cage getting an electric shock when he pushes open the wrong door and a tidbit of food when he opens the right one? The rat soon learns the rules of his reward-retribution game. But humans are not rats, and the game is much more complex.

This was the issue raised by the book of Job. Shall man serve God because he fears punishment if he does not, or does God merit our service regardless of the consequence? Shall man serve God in order to get God's blessing, or is obedience a worthy end in itself, regardless of reward? Or turn the issue around and look at it from the end of event and circumstance. Are these simply consequences of a good or an evil life? Can we observe a man's experience—what has happened to him, whether painful or pleasurable—and tell what kind of life he has lived? In short, is there any alternative to believing that God is indifferent or helpless in the face of innocent suffering, or that those suffering are really not innocent but getting what they deserve?

The book of Job will disappoint the person searching for a

proof-text answer to such profound issues. Indeed, Job is a passionate rejection of superficial explanations of the mystery of human suffering. But it is by no means a hand-wringing exercise on the futility of trying to cope. It is a resounding affirmation of God's sovereignty and righteousness, and an unequivocal rejection of the doctrine that life "evens up" here on earth. Its basic question is, What does it mean to be a man of faith? Not rational argument, but the experience of encountering God in the midst of life, leads to these inquiries. Job does not tell us everything about God. Nobody has except him who said, "He who has seen me has seen the Father" (John 14:9). But Job does reassure us that suffering need not be understood as evidence of God's disfavor, that out of the mystery swirling around us like a whirlwind the voice of God may be heard. Moreover, he holds that man is called to faithfulness to God without a guaranteed immunity from the hurt that goes with being human.

Since no thoughtful person escapes the necessity to grapple with the problems raised by Job its fascination is not surprising. Thomas Carlyle called it "a Noble Book; all men's Book! . . ." and added, "There is nothing written, I think, in the Bible or out of it, of equal literary merit." But it is not literary merit alone that gives Job its appeal. Rather, it is its accurate reflection of man's experience. No man is as morally upright as Job, and few suffer as intensely as he, but every man sooner or later asks "Why?" When he does he finds Job to be a companion.

The Origins of Wisdom in Israel's Life

The book of Job belongs to a type of literature known as Wisdom, common in the Near East, a special kind of writing based upon practical observations concerning the best way to live. But wisdom goes back much further in Israel's history. At its earliest level and in its most common usage, wisdom meant technical skill, manual dexterity, craftiness, "know-how." Wisdom was the art of achieving. The emphasis was on competence. "How to be successful, how to cope" was the essence of *hokmah*. Basically, then, wisdom could be largely secular, even non-ethical.

It might be the ability to perform well as a sailor, soldier, silversmith, midwife, mourner, or whatever. Examples of this mundane usage of wisdom abound in the Old Testament, some of which may be seen in Exodus 28:3; 35:25; 36:4; 2 Samuel 13:3; 1 Kings 2:6 (in which David instructs Solomon to use his wisdom in disposing of certain enemies); 1 Chronicles 22:15; 2 Chronicles 2:6,12; Isaiah 40:20; Jeremiah 10:9; Ezekiel 27:8-9.

Gradually the "wise" came to be a separate order, set alongside priesthood and prophethood, representing one of the official ways of serving the Lord. The priest served as teacher, liturgist, and administrator, including the supervision of worship and sacrifice. The prophet's work was by nature revelatory and interpretative. "Thus saith the Lord" was his mandate, as he brought the truth of God to bear upon his contemporary situation. But in addition to priest and prophet there was a third order in Israel's religious life—the wise. He was often secretary, counselor, and advisor to the court (2 Sam. 8:16-18; 1 Chron. 27:32-34). His trade was *hokmah,* wisdom, best understood as the art of making good decisions. The wise would say: "I have surveyed the human scene, and out of my experience, I tell you that this is the right way to act."

The prophets did not always approve of the wise, believing that the "how-life-works" approach to decision-making frequently left God out of the process. Men tended to reach conclusions based solely on observation and then to exalt their own cleverness instead of honoring God. The "prophet-prince" Isaiah, high in the councils of Judah's kings in the latter half of the eighth century B.C., sees the "wise" as threats to true prophetic religion. The wise tend to "pooh-pooh" the warnings and recommendations of the prophets (Isa. 5:19) and are often guilty of moral neutrality and ethical flexibility (v. 20), while being "wise in their own eyes" (v. 21). Isaiah's distrust of the court counselors is reflected also in 29:14-16; 30:1-5; 31:1-3. The prophet Jeremiah voices a similar distrust of the wise (8:8-9) and, for that matter, of most of Judah's leadership in his late seventh-century time (see Jer. 9:22-23; 18:18).

Wisdom Literature in the Old Testament

Not enough has been made of Wisdom writing in the Old Testament. Law, History, and Prophecy are much better known. But three books of the Old Testament—Job, Proverbs, Ecclesiastes—and Psalms 1,34,37,49,73,112,127-129,133 belong to Wisdom. In addition, two of the books of the Apocrypha, accepted by the Roman Catholic Church as Scripture and revered by many Protestants as well, are Wisdom writing. These are the Wisdom of Jesus the Son of Sirach (also called Ecclesiasticus) and the Wisdom of Solomon.

Wisdom writing in the Old Testament is customarily poetic in form. What distinguishes it, however, is its content. It is written in the form of observations on life. It is the distillation of human experience. It is commonsense religion. But there is a wide spectrum of understanding about life seen in the Wisdom books. For instance, the book of Proverbs announces a kind of pragmatic morality, that is, we get what is coming to us. Do good and you prosper; do evil and you suffer. The book of Job, on the other hand, raises objections to such a prudential view. Yet both books belong to Wisdom Literature, for their positions are based upon the reasoned examination of the evidence of experience.

As the Law is associated with the name of Moses and the Psalms with the name of David, so Solomon is the symbol of Wisdom. First Kings 3 and 4 extol Solomon's wisdom as having "surpassed the wisdom of all the people of the east, and all the wisdom of Egypt" (4:30). That reference, incidentally, alludes to the now commonly known fact that wisdom was not a phenomenon peculiar to Israel, but characteristic of the writing of Egypt, Babylonia, Edom, and others of Israel's neighbors. Wisdom surely antedates Solomon, as the fable of the thorn bush in Judges 9:7-21 illustrates, but in his reign it flowered. Under Solomon, a great patron of the arts, wisdom received strong impetus. Indeed, the historian in 1 Kings declares that "he also uttered three thousand proverbs; and his songs were a thousand and five" (4:32).

Further, Wisdom writing is characterized by its primary concern with the individual. While the Law and the Prophets certainly did not disregard the individual with his rights and responsibilities, they placed the nation in the center of their concern. Both viewed the relationship of Israel to God mainly as a corporate matter, the welfare of the individual being realized in the wellbeing of the nation. When the prophets spoke of sin and judgment, they were decrying individual sins, to be sure, but they saw these sins as bringing disaster upon the nation. Israel was a "people of God," not just a nation of individuals each of whom had his own separate relationship with God.

Individualism in Israel was brought into focus by the disaster of the Babylonian Exile in the sixth century, B.C. This shattering experience required a reevaluation of the belief in solidarity. Jeremiah, often called "the father of religious individualism," and his contemporary, Ezekiel, were two prophetic voices at the time of the Exile who raised questions about the "one-for-all-and-all-for-one" doctrine. Both denied the validity of an accepted proverb which expressed the belief: "The fathers have eaten sour grapes, and the children's teeth are set on edge." Jeremiah (31:29-34) went on to announce a new covenant written on the human heart. Ezekiel held that every man will be judged according to his own deeds, that he cannot blame others for his sin or its consequences. These are important declarations of individualism, but it is to the Wisdom writers in the Old Testament that we are chiefly indebted for concern about the individual and his welfare.

Early Hebrew Wisdom writing was occasionally in the form of a fable (as noted above), or a riddle (see Judg. 14:12-18), but ordinarily in the form of a proverb—a brief, pithy, sensible, rememberable maxim distilling the reflections and conclusions of countless generations in the tireless search for the "art of living." The book of Proverbs is the primary example of this type of wisdom in the Old Testament.

The book of Job belongs to this body of writing—Wisdom—but it is quite different in approach from the book of Proverbs. Proverbs are brief declarations, positive or negative, reporting a conclusion. The books of Job and Ecclesiastes, and certain of the psalms (see 49 and 73) reflect a speculative, questioning, somewhat philosophical approach to the great problems of human existence. They, too, are Wisdom, but their mood is more interrogative than declarative. They do not have short answers to complex qustions. That should not be taken to mean that this kind of Wisdom writing, of which Job is the finest example, has nothing to affirm about God. Rather, it is to say that in these writings we have a drastic challenge to those conclusions about life which seem unaware of the mystery surrounding it. In short, there are two strains of Wisdom in the Old Testament. One is prudential and didactic, instructing the reader on the practical duties of a well-ordered life. The other is speculative and philosophical, commenting on the perennial questions of man about the meaning of existence. Both approach life from the view of human experience.

Generally speaking, Wisdom writing in the form of short, pithy comments on practical morality is earlier. Large sections of Proverbs (10:1 to 22:17; 24:1 to 29:27) are attributed to Solomon, tenth century B.C. The later Proverbs (see chs. 1-9), while retaining the epigrammatic and didactic style, are apt to be in the form of somewhat lengthy discourses on such subjects as wisdom being an expression of the mind of God, the values of marital love and fidelity, and warnings against common pitfalls into sin. There does appear to be a development from the practical to the philosophical in wisdom. Job and Ecclesiastes belong to this flowering period of Hebrew wisdom.

Origin of Job

Having seen Job as an important aspect of a particular segment of the Old Testament, we turn now to the book itself. The origin of the writing is not known. As there is nothing in the book fixing its date with certainty, a great variety of opinion has been expressed on that subject. Writes one commentator, "Rabbinic opinions as to the date of the book of Job range from the era of the patriarchs (ca. 2100-1550 B.C.) down to the

Persian period."[1]

The question of the age of the book must not be confused with that of the age of Job himself. Job is represented in the book as living in patriarchal times. Like the great forefathers of Israel, he is rich in cattle and flocks (1:3; 42:12). Also as a patriarch, Job, as the head of the family, is its priest and offers sacrifice (1:5; 42:8). The advanced age to which Job lived is patriarchal (42:16). The musical instruments named are the simple ones of primitive times (21:12; 30:31). Most of these references are in either the Prologue or the Epilogue of the book. This suggests that at least the basic story of Job, a righteous man who suffered incredible disasters and then in the end was restored in health, happiness, and fortune, reaches far back into the patriarchal period.

There are two scriptural references to Job outside the book, one in Ezekiel 14:14,20, where he is mentioned along with Noah and Daniel as examples of righteous men whom God would honor and save. Ezekiel was preaching the doctrine of individual responsibility and cited the three to argue that though exemplary themselves, they could provide no merit for others. The other reference to Job is in the New Testament, James 5:11, where Job's "steadfastness" is cited. The reference from Ezekiel tells us only that "Job" was a recognized example of righteousness when this book was written about the time of the Babylonian captivity (6th century B.C.). The reference in James appears not to take account of the desperation of Job throughout most of the book. Both scriptural references indicate the antiquity of the story of Job.

Turn now to another line of evidence, the similarities between the biblical Job and righteous sufferers in stories which had currency among some of Israel's neighbors.[2] Literary parallels between the biblical Job and certain Near Eastern stories are believed by many scholars to be demonstrable. Among these are Egyptian poems such as "Complaint of the Eloquent Peasant," and "Dialogue About Human Misery." These documents show no dependency on or derivation from the book of Job or vice versa, but they do reveal a concern with some of the same questions that come to light in Job.

A more striking similarity is found in a Babylonian poem called, after its first line, "I Will Praise the Lord of Wisdom." This poem, of which about one half survives, has sometimes been called "The Babylonian Job." It is about a righteous sufferer who has had great wealth and honor only to lose it all. The poem reflects upon the mystery of such a happening. There are resemblances to Job but also striking differences. One of the differences is that the Babylonian hero, unlike Job, admits that he must have been guilty of some unknown sin and his problem is to discover what it is. The suffering of the righteous has been a subject of general examination in Near Eastern thought, although no direct relationship between the biblical Job and wisdom writings of other peoples can be established.

The setting of the biblical Job provides another interesting facet of the problem of origin. The scene of the book is outside the land of Israel. He lived in Uz, most likely Edom, southeast of Israel (see Gen. 36:28; Lam. 4:21). Job is "the greatest of all the people of the east" (Job 1:3). The "sons of the East" are in Judges 6:3,33; 7:12; 8:10, and elsewhere, identified with Midianites and Amalekites from east of the Jordan River. Moreover, Job's three friends are not from Israel. Eliphaz and Bildad are almost certainly Edomites, and Zophar's origin is obscure. The Sabeans (1:15) and Chaldeans (1:17) are likely Arab raiding parties who preyed upon their neighbors from time immemorial. The evidence suggests a story of common currency and antiquity which has become the vehicle of one of the great pieces of God's revelation in the Bible.

We have been circling the book of Job in search of evidence about its origin. Now we must look within it, at the language, and ideas. Many Aramaic words, grammatical forms, and constructions are found in the text. This fact strongly suggests a post-Exilic date for the writing, for it was in the Babylonian Exile that the spoken language of the Hebrews became Aramaic. Further, this type of Wisdom, speculative and philosophical, is believed to be largely a post-Exilic phenomenon. The tragic events of the Exile had been grappled with in the circles of the wise as they sought to understand the mysteries of a righteous God who permits evil to exist and good people to suffer. Indeed, Judah's catastrophe in the Exile makes an appropriate backdrop for the examination of the dire tragedy of Job. One passage (12:17 ff.) reads like an eyewitness account of the Babylonian captivity.

A post-Exilic date for the writing of the book is viewed as most likely by numerous Old Testament scholars of importance. Among them are A. B. Davidson (who sees striking similarities between the figure of Job and that of the Suffering Servant of the Babylonian captivity section of Isaiah), Driver and Gray, H. W. Robinson, Terrien, Kissane, and Gordis.[3]

This writer's conclusion is that the author of the book of Job belonged to post-Exilic Judaism, that he took the character of an ancient hero celebrated for both his righteousness and his suffering, and from that story which had common currency in the Near East, he wrote this divinely inspired poem.

Structure and Outline

The book of Job as a literary work alone merits study. It is a masterpiece of Hebrew literary genius whose structure is intriguing. The book opens and closes with prose statements describing the condition of the hero. Chapters 1 and 2 comprise a Prologue in which the circumstances under which the theological questions to be examined are stated. Here we have a man wholly upright. He is no common man, but classic man, man as he should be but is not. Now subject him to a series of terrible catastrophes and then wrestle with the question, "Why should a man do right, anyway? Is there any 'percentage' in it?" You have now set the stage. See what happens.

What follows is not the unfolding of a drama full of action, event, or happening. Instead it is a poem in which several great issues that relate to the righteousness of God and the mystery of human suffering are exposed by means of conversations between the principals in the poem. There is no "movement," except in the intensity of the feeling and thought expressed, until the poem comes to a crescendo with the voice of Yahweh speaking from a whirlwind.

There are three cycles of dialogue between Job and his three friends, beginning with chapter 3, an opening soliloquy by the suffering hero. Each cycle consists of a speech by each one of the three and a reply to each by Job, except in the third where, as it now appears, there are speeches from only two friends and two replies by Job. There are some textual problems in the book, this being one of them, which will be examined as the text is studied. The chapters encompassing the three cycles are: First cycle, 3-14; second cycle, 15-21; third cycle, 22-31.

Chapters 31-37 are an interesting and sometimes humorous interlude in which a young critic, Elihu, hitherto unknown in the book, injects himself with great gusto and emotion. The Elihu section does not add significantly to the issues being raised, although he does speak to the problem. Then almost abruptly, without further word from Job, Yahweh speaks. God challenges Job and, whereas his friends could give him no satisfaction, he is silenced by the Almighty. All he can do is to voice his repentance. This is the substance of chapters 38 to 42:6.

A brief prose Epilogue (42:7-17) closes the book. In it Job's fortunes are restored double-fold, and his friends are rebuked. The prose character of the Prologue and Epilogue, as distinguished from the poetic form of the main body, has suggested to many scholars that the Prologue-Epilogue prose is earlier in origin than the poem.

But whether there is one or a half-dozen sources of the material is not crucial if one believes that through this vehicle God speaks his infallible Word.

CHAPTER 2
The Basic Issue

Can a case be made for pure love which is without calculation of possible reward? Or are we finally reduced to acknowledging Satan's cynicism that there is no such thing as unstudied and unselfish goodness? "Does Job fear God for nought" (1:9) is his obscene counter to the Almighty's suggestion that Job was an example of man-at-his-best, one blameless and upright, reverencing God and shunning evil.

"Why not?" is the Adversary's sardonic reply. "Who wouldn't serve you faithfully in exchange for such goods? You have put a protective hedge about him. He has all the human heart could desire—health, wealth, and a large family. No wonder he serves you. He would be a fool to trifle with such beneficence. But if you really think that Job does this freely and only because he believes it is right, you are more gullible than I. Sweep all of this away, reduce him to the bare level of existence, and you will see a man who, no longer having a reason to bow and scrape before you, will curse you to your face."

It is a challenge that could not be ignored, for it strikes at the heart of conventional religion and morality. In spite of all evidence in Scripture and experience to the contrary, this type of religion continues to be widely accepted. Its propositions run: (1) God, being just, must surely reward the righteous and punish the wicked, else there is no difference between the two and therefore the entire moral order is questionable. (2) A man prosperous in life and goods surely gives evidence of being rewarded, and inasmuch as God is in control of this world we may presume that God has found such a man worthy, bestowing blessings consonant with his worthiness. (3) Contrariwise, one who has not done well may not expect God's blessings, and therefore, if you want to get along in this world you will be a good fellow and obey God. The natural outcome of such reasoning is the strong temptation to turn religion into a pious pragmatism. So, Satan said, remove Job's motive for serving God—material blessing—and he will be no more pious than the next man. Like a disappointed relative, he will curse your name when he discovers that he has been left out of your will.

Pragmatic religion is a persistent and insidious heresy. It is so because of its plausibility. There is blessedness in doing right. But it is a far different thing to imply that doing right guarantees bliss. From there it is only a short but fatal step to the attempt to manipulate God and put him in one's debt for doing right. Must religion always become in the end a means of getting God on our side? Is morality the coin that buys blessedness? Is being devout "the best policy?" Or does man serve the Lord God Almighty because it is his right and duty to do so, regardless of the consequence? It is one of the important questions of religion in all times, and it is the basic issue of the book of Job.

Other issues arise in the book. It is common to suppose that the crucial problem is the justification of God in the face of the fact of innocent suffering. How can one believe in a righteous God in a world like this? It is a question that must be spoken to, it cannot be ignored. But the book of Job does not answer it. Job, the innocent sufferer, is never told why he suffered. Yet he is satisfied, for he makes a discovery so great that it swallows up the mystery with a profound affirmation. He finds God. Where and how this experience takes place is another of the cardinal issues of the book.

Job also wrestles with the personal problem of his survival of death. But this concern is even less central than that of innocent suffering. The author raises the question and expresses the hope that if a man die he shall live again (14:14), but it is only a glimmer in the book of Job. For the most part, he shares the view of his contemporaries that man's life is brought down to

Sheol, the abode of the dead. The beginnings of the hope of resurrection are in Job, looking forward to a glorious fulfilment in Christ, but they are only beginnings.

There is also the clear recognition in Job that man cannot save himself. His justification lies elsewhere. Thus he longs for a defender, an advocate, a redeemer who will stand up for him and plead his cause. We Christians are quick to identify the Redeemer. We know for whom Job longs. But we must always be honest with the text and not read into it a meaning which was not there. We can say that the text is fulfilled in Christ. But honesty compels us not to load Job with greater theological freight than he is meant to carry. We do not suggest that there is no connection between the book of Job and the New Testament; there is, in our Christian view, a fulfilment of the former in the latter. But we do intend to avoid impressing upon Job an understanding which has come to us because we stand on this side of the historic Christ and see the book in his light.

Reward and Retribution

The fact that this question should be raised by this writer perhaps in the fifth century B.C., is in itself remarkable. Throughout much of the religious history of Israel it was held that God, being just, meted out retribution and reward in exact proportion to man's deserving. The doctrine that God will render to every man according to his works (Matt. 16:27; Rom. 2:6; 1 Cor. 3:8) is compatible with Christian faith because of the belief in the final judgment and life after death.

But, as has been noted above, until late pre-Christian Judaism the belief regarding life after death was that all went to Sheol, a shadowy existence where good and evil alike lived without distinction (see Job 3:11-19; 14:7-12; 21:22-26; 30:23). Reward and retribution occurred in this life, for God is just and rewards the righteous while punishing the wicked.

There was little occasion for questioning the doctrine as long as retribution was considered primarily in terms of the corporate body of the nation Israel. Deuteronomy 28 is a classic statement of the doctrine. Yahweh promises rewards of prosperity and protection to Israel if she will be obedient to the Covenant, but punishment and defeat by her enemies if she is not. The books of Judges, Samuel, and Kings illustrate the working out of the law of reward and retribution in Israel's history. Of course, the innocent sometimes suffered with the guilty, for they were members of the same sinful group.

With the Babylonian Exile came greater emphasis on individualism and the prophets and Wisdom writers began to reinterpret the doctrine of exact reward or retribution. There was, of course, the sentiment expressed in the Wisdom psalm: "I have been young, and now am old; yet I have not seen the righteous forsaken or his children begging bread" (37:25). And there was the prophet Ezekiel at the time of the Exile, holding out for a strict individualism (always a one-sided view of the human situation, for no one is only an individual), saying that when a man eats "sour grapes" he sets his own "teeth on edge," not his children's. But in the main, the simplistic explanation that each man gets what is coming to him was being modified by Israel's confrontation with the facts of life.

Jeremiah, Ezekiel's contemporary, believed no less than he in individual responsibility. To him that made the prosperity of the wicked and the suffering of the righteous all the more mystifying (Jer. 12:1-3). Isaiah of the Babylonian Exile saw the same terrible events of Jerusalem's fall and destruction, the humiliation of her best people, and her loss of national identity. How could one understand? Surely even Judah's worst was better than Babylon's best. She had "received from the Lord's hand double for all her sins" (Isa. 40:2). This great prophet can understand and accept the plight of God's people only by viewing it as a kind of "over and above" payment, not alone for her sins, but for others' as well. Vicarious suffering is seen as the only adequate explanation of what Judah has endured. So one who suffers on behalf of others, the Suffering Servant, becomes the model of the noblest understanding of suffering.

Others, seeing the apparent disparity between righteousness and reward in this life, reconciled it by holding that the success of the wicked was only temporary. Thus the writer of Psalm 73 (a Wisdom Psalm), depressed and perplexed by the arrogance of wicked scoffers, is about to decide that "all in vain have I kept my heart clean and washed my hands in innocence" (v. 13). But then he goes into the sanctuary of God and perceives the end of the wicked. Suddenly, in a moment, they would be swept away. In a similar vein, Zophar, one of Job's friends, tells him that evil-doing is like a piece of sweet-tasting food which a man holds in his mouth, savoring its delight as long as possible. But when he swallows it, it turns his stomach like gall and he has to vomit it up (Job 20:12-15,KJV). Others said, "Perhaps the wicked do escape punishment, but 'God stores up their iniquity for their sons'" (see 21:19). But Job will not accept that explanation, for it makes him doubt the justice of God. What kind of God would take out his wrath on the innocent children of an unrighteous man?

Some sought to resolve the problem of a just God who permits the wicked to prosper and the righteous to suffer by interpreting suffering as a blessing in disguise. Through suffering God is seeking either to test or to teach us. God tested Abraham by telling him to sacrifice his son Isaac (Gen. 22). Similarly, Satan is allowed free rein to bring Job to ruin and humiliation to prove whether or not he serves God for what he gets out of it or for nobler reasons. Or if God is not testing, he is teaching the sufferer. We learn much from what we suffer. The writer of the letter to the Hebrews gives the ultimate example of unmerited suffering as discipline, applying it to Christ himself: "Although he was a Son, he learned obedience through what he suffered" (5:8). So if you are being disciplined by God he is treating you as a son. Therefore (here he quotes Prov. 3:11) "Do not regard lightly the discipline of the Lord" (Heb. 12:5).

It is only with the establishment of the belief in life after death that the question of reward and retribution finds a satisfactory answer. The facts belie the notion that in this life we get what we deserve. But if we believe that there is an eternal destiny for man, and that his life here has everlasting consequences, then the justice of God is seen in vastly larger context. In Job there is no firm belief in life after death, although hope and longing for it are expressed. It is because we know of Christ's empty tomb that we say with Paul's confidence: "There is laid up for me the crown of righteousness, which the Lord, the righteous judge, will award me on that day" (2 Tim. 4:8).

Jesus refined the reward-retribution doctrine, instead of rejecting it. He did reject the notion that misfortune must be attributed to judgment upon sin. This is plain in his interpretation of the tragedy of some Galileans slaughtered by Pilate's troops, and the misfortune of eighteen people killed in the collapse of a building (Luke 13:1-5). It is clear also in his response to the disciples' question about a man who had been born blind (John 9:3). He was not squeamish about rewards and punishments, as a reading of Matthew 6:1-18; 25:14-30,31-40, as well as many other passages reporting his sayings will show. But he did not believe in material reward for spiritual service. He did believe in rewards and, as a contemporary New Testament scholar puts it, "We ought to be careful that we do not try to be more spiritual than Jesus was in our thinking about this matter of reward."[1]

How the Problem Is Treated in Job

The doctrine that man receives his just due in this life is challenged in Job by the simple device of offering an exception. This becomes evident in the opening words where an idealized picture of human nature is given. Job was "perfect," a finished product, the complete man. He reverenced God and avoided all evil (1:1), and also showed a godly father's concern for the spiritual condition of his children (v. 5). Job's uprightness was not simply a matter of his public reputation, but also the judgment of God about him (v. 8; 2:3). The writer of Job has provided us with a classic case. Suppose a man "blameless and upright," is subjected to utter devastation, how will he react? What will this case do to the doctrine that uprightness is rewarded and evil is punished in this life?

No ordinary man will do, for he might be suspected of some secret sin which when exposed makes his suffering deserved. It is precisely this which his friends suspect. "Remember, I pray thee," says Eliphaz, "who ever perished, being innocent?" (4:7, KJV). "If thou wert pure and upright," Bildad accuses, "surely now he would awake for thee, and make the habitation of thy righteousness properous" (8:6, KJV). "Thou hast said, My doctrine is pure, and I am clean in thine eyes," sneers Zophar, "but oh that God would speak, and open his lips against thee" (11:4-5, KJV). But the point is that we really do have an upright man here who is suffering incredible misfortune.

Now, according to the doctrine of retribution and reward, that should not happen. Job's friends did not believe it would happen. Job had not believed it, either. Both Job and his friends at the beginning of the book represent the same point of view, the standard one that reward follows righteousness, retribution wickedness. Because they do believe this the friends are certain that Job is guilty. But because Job is certain that he is innocent he is finding it impossible to believe the doctrine any more. It may be true in general, but there have to be exceptions—Job is one.

The Prologue sets forth the case in clean, swift strokes. First, there is the presentation of the hero, Job, a man of Edom (1:1-5). This is followed by picturing a scene in heaven in which Yahweh is seen as a royal Potentate before whom the "sons of God" present themselves. "The Satan" also comes. Note the use of the definite article, suggesting that the term is a title and not yet a proper name. The figure here does not suggest the fully developed character of the personification of evil in later Jewish and Christian doctrine concerning "Satan" or "devil." He is "the Adversary," still reporting to Yahweh at his court, but not as one of the "sons of God." That his intentions are evil, however, there is no doubt. In sly innuendo he suggests that Job's remarkable piety is only a form of enlightened self-interest. "Does Job serve God for nothing?"

It is a waste of time to attempt to rationalize Yahweh's "taking the dare" of the Adversary that the Lord's prize subject, Job, would change his tune if his benefits were withdrawn. It is a magnificent parable, told with consummate artistry, the scene shifting back and forth from the glory of the heavenly court to the terror of Job's earthly disasters. Note, for example, the writer's deft way of showing the Adversary's impudence when Yahweh asks him where he has been. He answers like a sullen teen-ager to his parent: "Oh, just around, going to and fro on the earth" (see 1:5; 2:2). Another example of the artistry is seen in the repeated use of the expression, "While he was yet speaking" (1:16,17,18) to emphasize the rapidity of the hammer-blows of disaster upon Job.

Job is put to the test, but he does not waver. In all that has happened he does not charge God with being in poor taste, or acting capriciously (v. 22). So the test is made more severe, for the Adversary says with characteristic cynicism that Job's life has not yet been touched at the quick, even though his children are all dead and his wealth is destroyed. "Skin for skin! All that a man has he will give for his life" (2:4). The words remind one of Jesus' saying, "What shall a man give in return for his life?" (Matt. 16:26). But there is a whole world of difference between the implications of the two. Job now is afflicted with a loathsome disease which turns his skin into a mass of repulsive, suppurating sores. Reduced to penury, childless, and completely broken in health, he takes his place on the town ash heap—literally, the sewage heap—where he sits scraping the pus from his sores with a piece of broken pottery.

When his wife, perhaps in mistaken pity, calls upon him to renounce God and accept with dignity the certain death of one who blasphemes, he rebukes her. She speaks as one of "the foolish women" (2:10), one of the *nabalim,* which does not mean simple, or innocent, or naive, but rather a vicious distorter, one who deliberately twists the truth. So now he is alone, but he will not "sin with his lips" (v. 10).

At this point the three friends are introduced. They get together and come to see Job, and are moved to great pity when they see him. His suffering has changed him beyond recognition. In silence they sit down with him seven days and nights. That was true friendship and genuine comfort. It was also the last comfort they were to give him. When they found out what he was think-ing they were dismayed, shocked, then outraged and incensed. He challenged a basic tenet of their religion, namely, that God rewards the good and punishes the wicked. Once Job had believed that himself. But now he saw that that doctrine did not cover all of the facts.

The scene is set for the great debate. The proposition is: Will man serve God simply because God is God and it is man's privilege to serve him, or has he the right to demand that God take care of him in exchange for trying to do right? Let us hear the argument.

CHAPTER 3
Job the Dissenter

The First Cycle of Dialogue (3:1 to 14:22)

The poem of Job begins with a soliloquy by the tortured hero, who would welcome death as a friend come to release him from the enemy. The anguish of one who asks to die because life has become unbearable makes us uneasy, perhaps even angry. We may feel threatened by his unrestrained challenge to the life-wish, being not so much afraid for him as for ourselves. Who has never entertained the wish to escape the terror of life by embracing the sweet fascination of death? The special appeal of Job is partly due to its transcript of the raw emotion of a man at wit's end responding with integrity.

His friends are moved—appalled at his appearance, shocked by his rebellion, terrified by his candor. Job breaks the long silence in which they have held vigil with him seven days and nights, but he addresses neither them nor God. It is the lament of a broken man lashing out at life. He asks no audience. Indeed, he is unaware of having one. He must simply drain some of the bitterness out of his heart. The cry of this deeply wounded man is expressed in the form of three wishes: that he had never been born (3:3-10); that he might have died at birth (vv. 11-19); that he might die now (vv. 20-26). The reference to the "knees" receiving him (v. 12) alludes to the practice of placing the newborn infant on the father's lap as a symbolic act of acceptance of the child's legitimacy. Verses 14-19 are an eloquent description of Sheol as conceived of in traditional Hebrew thought until very near the beginning of the Christian era. In the concluding section (3:20-26), Job introduces the idea that God is responsible for his plight. God has hedged him in (v. 23). It is only the beginning of his accusation, but it suggests that he may become something less than "patient Job."

Eliphaz the Mystic: First Speech (4:1 to 5:27)

The first of Job's three friends bases his belief in traditional reward and retribution on mystical experience. There are three speeches in the dialogue assigned to him, chapters 4 and 5 comprising the first. This initial effort is well-organized and moves logically to the conclusion that God is just and therefore Job should not be impatient but trust that everything will turn out well. To a man who has lost everything, including his entire family, that may not be helpful.

Eliphaz begins politely, but with a mild rebuke to the sufferer for collapsing when trouble came to him. He had comforted others, now he couldn't take it himself (4:1-5)! Verse 6 contains a veiled hint that Job may not be as innocent as he claims to be. If he is innocent, then he has nothing to worry about; his reverence of God and his personal integrity guarantee God's eventual favor. Next, in verses 7-11, Eliphaz mouths the pious platitude that "the good guy always wins." "Think now, who that was innocent ever perished?" (4:7). Once Job would have accepted that doctrine without equivocation. Eliphaz's appeal at this point is to God's law of sowing and reaping (4:8). If you sow, you reap. This is a doctrine approved by Jesus (Matt. 7:16), but he never used it to explain the mystery of innocent suffering, or the equally anomalous situation of the happiness and prosperity of the wicked. But Eliphaz is spokesman for a view which requires that Job be guilty in order to explain his suffering.

Having made a claim on the basis of dogma, Eliphaz next makes one on the basis of supernatural revelation (Job 4:12-21). In the silence of the night he had had a vision, "a spirit glided past my face" (v. 15), and a voice spoke: "Can mortal man be righteous before [KJV, "more just than"] God?" (v. 17). Job might look good by comparison with others, but in the light of God's holiness, he can lay no claim to innocence. This, of course, is true but it does not get us anywhere, for it only says that all human virtue is relative, and does not tell us why one man who is relatively purer than others still suffers more.

Having stated the dogma and argued for it on the basis of supernatural revelation, Eliphaz next contends that only a fool would question the justice of his lot in life (5:1-7). Since all men are sinners, what right has the sufferer to resent God when his sins catch up with him? The thought concludes with that familiar—and misinterpreted—verse (7) that "man is born unto trouble, as the sparks fly upward." The verse really says that man "begets trouble," brings it on himself, as certainly as the sparks fly upward. Verse 6 immediately preceding this one makes the meaning plain.

In verses 8-16 Eliphaz implores Job to turn his cause over to God in the confidence that God always does the best thing. The presumption is that Job's suffering in some way fulfils God's intention. Therefore, it is wicked and unwise not to submit. God "pays off" and there is no escaping his judgment.

The concluding section of Eliphaz's opening counsel to Job (vv. 17-27) is a pious homily appealing to the sufferer to "despise not the chastening of the Almighty" (v. 17). With shallow sympathy he turns upon his friend, beaten into the earth by the hammerblows of disaster, and says brightly, "Don't worry, everything is for the best." He promises Job that his suffering is only a temporary disciplinary measure instituted by the Almighty, and that all kinds of good things would happen to him if he would just trust. The closing admonition is the epitome of a loveless orthodoxy: "Hear, and know it for your good" (v. 27). Whenever somebody says, "I am telling you this for your own good," watch out.

Job's Reply to Eliphaz (6:1 to 7:21)

The moralistic admonitions of Eliphaz have not helped the sufferer to accept his situation. Do they ever? Job needed consolation. He got advice. His reply to Eliphaz, comprising chapters 6 and 7, reflects his disappointment with his friend's failure to understand the depth of his travail. It falls into three parts: an opening lament (6:1-13); a rebuke to the three friends for their failure to support him in his hour of trial (6:14 to 7:6); and a prayer to God asking the Almighty to help him (7:7-21).

In the opening words Job expresses in a beautiful metaphor the weight of his burden. He says that if laid in the balance it would be heavier than the sand of the sea. For the first time Job implicates God as being responsible for his affliction (v. 4). That is the heaviest burden of all, and is the reason for the rashness of his words (v. 3). It is as natural to protest when you are unjustly wounded as it is for the wild ass to bray or the ox to low when hungry (v. 5), or for man to gag over insipid food (v. 6). This somewhat obscure reference to the tastelessness of certain foods may be an indirect reference to the tasteless speech of Eliphaz. In any event, Job feels that his agitation of heart is wholly justified, and he wishes that God would go ahead and strike him and have it over with (vv. 8-9). If so, at least he would have the consolation of knowing that he had been loyal to God to the end despite his suffering (v. 10). He concludes this thought with a bitter rejection of the suggestions of Eliphaz (5:8,17) that he should patiently accept what comes. Why should I be patient? he asks. What am I, some kind of stone or bronze statue? Have I no human feelings (vv. 11-12)?

It is a terrible thing to lose confidence in one's friends, but Job finds himself in that position (6:14 to 7:6). To withhold kindness from a friend is to turn one's back on true religion (6:14). Job's friends have done just that. They are like a torrential stream overflowing in the rainy season, but dried up when needed by the thirsty caravan in the parching summer heat (vv. 15-20). They see his calamity and are uneasy and fearful (v. 21). Who has not felt that embarrassing discomfort in the presence of another's grief? The more Job thinks about them the angrier he becomes, shouting: "Make me understand!" (v. 24).

Perhaps at this point they were offended and turned to leave, and Job, sensing that he has said too much, pleads with them: "Please look at me. Don't leave, for my very life is at stake" (see vv. 28-29). In something of a conciliatory tone he then addresses them concerning the hopelessness of man's estate, illustrating by his own (7:1-6). He says that the nights are long (v. 4) and the days "swifter than a weaver's shuttle" (v. 6). How like life that is! When you are lonely and afraid the time drags interminably, but when you think of life as a whole it seems to get away from you before you realize it.

The final section of Job's reply to Eliphaz is a prayer to God (7:7-21). It begins with a statement of the brevity and fragility of human life (vv. 7-10). If God does not soon repair the damage done to Job it will be too late. This is his justification for speaking so boldly of his bitterness to the Almighty (v. 11). The heart of the prayer is that God should have no cause to pick on Job. Verses 17 and 18 are almost a duplication of Psalm 8:4, with an opposite conclusion. The psalmist is moved to wonder that God, maker of heaven and earth, takes an interest in man. Job says in effect, "Don't you have enough to do running the universe, or must you always intrude yourself into my affairs?" If man sins, why should that concern the Creator of the universe (7:20-21)? Is it so great a thing to God? Here is one of the great issues in the Bible. We do not have a God who is satisfied with the order in the universe. The truly great news of the gospel is that he is very much concerned with what happens to each one of us. As yet Job is unable to face that truth.

Bildad the Traditionalist: First Speech (8:1-22)

Whereas Eliphaz had argued from the basis of mystical experience, the second friend, Bildad, using primarily the same argument, appeals to tradition. He opens with a salvo fired at Job's most vulnerable spot, his fatherly concern for his children. The preliminary politeness of Oriental etiquette is laid aside; Bildad attacks. God cannot be perverse, he says, and therefore Job and his children must be guilty. The suggestion that the children had sinned (v. 4), receiving their just due, must have hurt deepest. But if Job will do two things—seek God and be pure and upright—God will rouse himself and come to the rescue

(v. 6). What a loveless and judgmental religion!

Bildad bases his arrogant judgment of such matters on history. Look back to bygone ages, he says. They will teach you that as surely as the papyrus plant can grow only in marshy soil or reeds only in the water, so certain is the ruin of those who forget God (vv. 8-11). Their fate may be delayed, but their security is only temporary and superficial. Sooner or later, consequences will overtake them (vv. 11-19). There is no arguing with Bildad's position, except to say that he clearly infers that when disaster strikes, as it had Job, it can only mean that God has finally said "Pay up." He has adjudged Job guilty, in spite of the sufferer's protestations to the contrary. Indeed, he closes his opening remarks with an appeal to Job to get right (vv. 20-22). God will still make everything right if Job will repent. Little wonder "patient Job" became so impatient.

Job's Appeal to the Sovereign, Irresistible God (9:1 to 10:22)

The ugly suggestion of Bildad that the dead children may have deserved what they got (8:4) is apparently ignored. Job is preoccupied with thoughts about God and man's relationship to him.

The opening section (9:1-13) deals with God's majesty and might. In a series of metaphors concerning the natural order, God's almightiness is affirmed: He removes mountains (v. 5), shakes the earth (v. 6), commands the sun and seals up the stars (v. 7), stretches out the heavens (v. 8), puts the constellations in their places (v. 9), and does great things beyond understanding (v. 10). No one can successfully challenge him. But God's power only makes Job feel more helpless. Though innocent, he can not argue with God.

He has no hope for justice but can only appeal for mercy (v. 15). This sounds for a moment like a foretaste of gospel, but then we realize that Job is not affirming that God is merciful. At this juncture he believes that God is simply irresistible. There is no way of getting acquittal based on a fair examination of the evidence. Verses 17-24 reveal the desperation of Job's condition.

God crushes him and multiplies his wounds without cause (v. 17). In a contest of strength or justice all the power is on God's side (v. 19). God laughs (RSV, mocks) at the calamity of the innocent (v. 23)! He alone must be regarded as responsible for what happens in this universe (v. 24). To say the least, those are not polite thoughts.

From outrage at the unequal contest between him and God, Job turns to plaintive reflection upon the brevity of his human life. In three vivid figures (9:25-26) he pictures the swift passing of his days, and then confesses that he is unable to convince himself to "cheer up" (vv. 27-28). He is hopelessly overmatched. This leads him to a second step (see 7:20-21) in his pilgrimage. It is the realization that since he is unable to justify himself, his only hope is for an "umpire" to arbitrate his cause (vv. 30-35). He sees God as the Invincible, Remote, Absolute One. If only there were a bridge between him and God! It is natural for Christians to see Job's longing as fully realized in Christ, although such a view of Christ is inadequate. He is Mediator, to be sure, but he has not come to "lay his hand upon" two adversaries—God on one side and man on the other. That is the way Job pictured it, but Christ was not here to appease God's anger. He came to be and to give God's love.

Since he has no umpire, Job returns to the challenge of God (10:1-22). His utter despair is expressed in the expletive: "I loathe my life" (9:21; 10:1). Is God enjoying his little game of cat and mouse with Job (v. 3)? Does God look with mortal eyes that are often mistaken (v. 4)? God's hands fashioned man from clay. Will he now break him up just for sport (vv. 8-12)? The complaint ends in a defiant challenge to God. Whether he does evil or good, it is the same. God pursues him like a lion after its prey, and therefore he asks only to be let alone to enjoy some peace and comfort for his few remaining days (vv. 13-22). Whatever else may be written of Job, we can no longer regard him as a patient, mild-mannered, long-suffering man. He is outraged and defiant at this point of his spiritual journey, and he does not hesitate to express himself.

Zophar the Dogmatist and Zealot: First Speech (11:1-20)

The third speaker minces no words. Job's outspoken criticism of God more than irrates Zophar—it infuriates him. He lashes out in a brief comment that expresses three thoughts. First (vv. 1-6), he announces that Job is obviously guilty and adds to his sin by the presumption of feigned innocence. Should Job, "a man full of talk" (v. 2) (literally, "a man of lips"), go unchallenged? Job is as guilty as sin; in fact, his suffering is less than his guilt deserves (v. 6)!

Next, Zophar affirms the doctrine of God's transcendence. He is utterly unknowable. Therefore, Job's effrontery in demanding that God "make sense" and explain himself is intolerable (vv. 7-12). Of course, Zophar is theoretically right. We can't plumb the depths of God or soar to his heights. We would not know him at all did he not choose to unveil himself to us. But it was a cold and cheerless dogmatism, doctrinally correct, but inexcusable. Finally, Zophar has the gall to make an appeal to the brokenhearted Job to repent and "set your heart aright" (v. 13), promising that if he will do so God will fill his life with good things (vv. 13-20). It was not so much what Zophar said which was offensive, but his thin-lipped gracelessness. Is it not often so with us that our zeal is spoiled by lovelessness?

Job's Reply to Zophar (12:1 to 14:22)

In this longest of Job's speeches of the first cycle we see him rising to sublime heights of hope only to fall back into the depths of despair. His words reflect the emotional inconsistency of the grief-stricken, apt in his raving to say both what he does not mean and things so profoundly meant that they probably would not be uttered in less uncontrolled moods. At times he speaks to the friends, at times to the Almighty. Although the mood of the speech varies, its thought falls into three divisions: An argument from experience against traditional dogma represented by the friends (12:1-25); an open challenge to friends and an open defiance of God (13:1-27); a longing for life eternal and final despair concerning it (13:28 to 14:22).

The three friends have now made their position clear. They represent the traditional belief in retributive justice. It is plain to Job that there is no way to convince them of his innocence. So he begins by setting himself in the position of the lonely dissenter. No doubt they represent the accepted view (12:2). Moreover, he recognizes that he is a laughingstock because he keeps denying the justice of his suffering, while they believe that his case proves the doctrine rather than disproving it (v. 4). Hard for Job to take is the brittle comment of these advisors blithely calling on him to accept the discipline of the Lord and repent. They who are at ease are full of good advice on how to handle adversity (v. 5)! But the fact is that no case can be made for an evenhanded justice in this world. Tents of robbers prosper, and idolaters (carrying their god around in their pocket) are secure (v. 6). Where is justice?

The power and sovereignty of God Job does not doubt. Nature testifies to it (12: 7-10). It is as logical as it is to conclude that the ear's purpose is hearing, the palate's tasting, and that wisdom comes with age (vv. 11-12). The passage following is a poem celebrating God's invincibility (vv. 13-25). Nobody successfully resists God. As noted earlier, there may be allusions here to the Babylonian Exile (see vv. 17-21,23). The passage agrees with and reinforces the argument of Zophar, perhaps intentionally so, for Job shortly remarks: "What you know, I also know; I am not inferior to you" (13:2). Job is conversant with all the classical arguments. But when your life is crushed arguments are vacuous and ineffective.

Job's impatience with the friends' words erupts in the fury of the lines of 13:1-12. He wants to speak to the Almighty, not to them, for he is weary of their pious phrases (v. 3). But before turning to challenge the Almighty he vents his hostility upon them. They are "worthless physicians" (v. 4) who lie for God in an effort to make God's case look good. Is God unable to defend himself (vv. 7-8)? Then with a strange but understandable inconsistency, Job warns the friends that God will punish them for their lying (vv. 10-12). He who doubts God's concern for justice is at the same time confident that God is just!

In the lines which follow we see another step in Job's spiritual journey. Nearly beside himself with grief and frustration he throws all caution to the winds. No one has heard him. The friends, at first diffidently and then bluntly, have expressed certainty of his guilt. God has not answered him. His case is hopeless anyway, so he will have his say. The familiar line in 13:15, "Though he slay me, yet will I trust in him" (KJV) is a beautiful thought concerning "faith at all cost," or a sublime "nevertheless," but it is not what the text reads in Job. The KJV reading has been taken from a marginal note in the Hebrew text. A study of this textual problem lies outside the scope of this work, but suffice it to say that the RSV reading, "Behold, he will slay me; I have no hope," not only fits the Hebrew text better but also is in harmony with the spirit of the passage. Job, believing that his case is hopeless, has decided to "tell it like it is," to "take my flesh in my teeth" (v. 14).

But the thought of his impending death paradoxically produces a momentary hope in him. The hope is based upon belief in his own innocence and the confidence that no godless man can stand before God. So his death may at last give him an opportunity to clear his name, for when God hears his case he will have to acquit him (13:15-19). So he turns to address God in prayer, requesting a confrontation (vv. 20-27). Two considerations are asked: That God "withdraw thy hand" (v. 21), for there can be no fair trial if the defendant is being coerced by torture; and that the "trial" be one in which both parties are heard (v. 22). Job is ready to be either "defendant" or "prosecutor," but he implores an opportunity for dialogue with the Almighty.

The third section of Job's reply to Zophar is in the form of longing for life eternal and a lapse into despair concerning its possibility (13:28 to 14:22). The section is introduced by comments on man's mortality. A cluster of beautiful metaphors is put together. Man is a moth-eaten garment (13:28), a flower that withers, a shadow that flees (14:2). Since he has such a short time, would it not be kinder for God to let him alone to enjoy his brief day like a hireling who wants no interference from his boss on his day off (v. 6).

Verses 7-12 dramatically state the finality of death. This view is eloquently put in the words, "So man lies down and rises not again; till the heavens are no more he will not awake . . ." (v. 12). But Job wishes that it were not so. There is no hope, but one must hope. Here we come upon one of the mountain peaks of this great book. Job, believing with his contemporaries in the end of life in Sheol, looks beyond his day to express a grand perhaps. Perhaps there is something beyond death. Is it just possible that God would hide his servant Job in Sheol until all the anger of God was past, then call him forth for communion (14:13-15)? Oh, what a great possibility! Job's heart leaps with longing. How eagerly he would answer such a call! "If a man die . . ." (v. 14). The death is certain, but "shall he live again?" Job's reason for entertaining such a possibility is not based upon dogma, but upon his personal feelings. He who loves God and believes in God can not resist the longing hope that one day he will stand before God and answer to his name.

But the end of Job's struggle is not yet. His soaring confidence soon sinks back into despair. It would be wonderful to believe that life is not ended by death, but he cannot believe it now. The speech concludes with the quiet despondency that there is nothing ahead but the end (vv. 18-22). Job's final judgment at this juncture is that God "destroyest the hope of man" (v. 19). Man lies in death; his sons come to mourn him, but he is unaware of their sorrow (v. 21). Indeed, in the final analysis, each of us is alone. As the first cycle comes to a close Job has soared high and then fallen back into a despair perhaps deeper than in his opening lament.

CHAPTER 4
Job the Defensive

The Second Cycle of Dialogue (15:1 to 21:34)

With the beginning of the second cycle there is a noticeable change in the temper of the friends' words. They had been severe but sympathetic and conciliatory. They had been shocked at his outbursts of indignation over his suffering, but had agreed at first that he had once set a good example before men, and they were confident that his repentence would yet bring restoration. However, Job had shown no disposition to repent, obstinately maintaining his innocence. Thus he had exposed himself to the fate of sinners. In the last two cycles there is little movement of the argument forward, but it goes in circular fashion, increasing in tempo and ferocity with every line. On his part, Job rejects their contention while alternating between hope of ultimate vindication and despair of ever seeing it.

The Second Speech of Eliphaz (15:1-35)

Politeness is forgotten (see 4:2-6). Eliphaz is more than ruffled; he is threatened by the sight of the noble sufferer who won't ask God's pardon. He strikes at him with a threefold attack. First, Job's speech betrays the inquity that lurks in his heart (15:2-6). Eliphaz's lines are meant to insult. A wise man (as Job holds himself to be) will not speak "windy knowledge" as if he has been feeding off of the hot, gusty, withering east wind. Further, Job is exercising a bad influence. "You are doing away with the fear of God" (v. 4). "You undermine religion," is the Moffatt translation. Why, Job's own words give him away, displaying his impiety (v. 6). Eliphaz was at this moment closer to Job's condition than he had been before. Job's suffering was not due to previous sin, but now his suffering is leading him to sin by falsely accusing God. Both the sufferer and his counselors had misunderstood man's relationship with God, supposing that virtue was rewarded with uninterrupted material blessing. It hadn't been, and Job was angry at God while they were sure that God was only doing his job by punishing the sinner.

Eliphaz continues with a second indictment (15:7-11), that Job has set himself up as a sort of expert on God. He acts as if he knows everything, despite the fact that he is a relatively young man in the presence of men older than his father. His lack of proper humility is an outrage. Third (15:12-16), Job has not only rejected the advice of his wise and older friends, but worse still, he has "turned . [his] spirit against God." At this point Eliphaz falls back on his previously expressed reasoning concerning man's comparative unrighteousness. "What is man, that he can be clean?" (v. 14). Eliphaz is right. No one is righteous. But Eliphaz is drawing the false conclusion that Job's suffering proves that God is punishing him.

The rest of Eliphaz's speech is designed to bring Job to his knees. It is a description of the fate of the wicked (15:17-35). The teaching of the wise men of old is that the wicked man suffers continual anxiety (vv. 17-21). Despite his prosperity he can't enjoy life because he knows that he is destined to die a miserable death. The day will come when he will have nothing (vv. 22-29). If disaster does not catch up with him personally it will strike his children, cutting off his posterity like unripe grapes dropping from the vine or an olive tree shedding its blossoms before the fruit forms (vv. 30-35). These last words are particularly cruel in the light of Job's tragic loss.

Job, Target for Divine Sport (16:1 to 17:16)

Job's replies are directed less and less to his counselors, whom he now feels do not understand. However, he does begin this second response to Eliphaz with a rebuke to these "miserable comforters" (16:2) who dare to identify their own shallow thoughts with the "consolations of God" (see 15:11). As Eliphaz had accused Job of answering with "windy knowledge" (15:2), so Job returns the compliment (16:3). Advice to the hurt is easy when you are not hurting! Job assures them that he could do as well at it as they if they could exchange places (16:4-5). His friends are no help, nor can he help himself, for neither speaking out nor remaining silent assuages the pain (16:6).

But the friends are not Job's burden. They only annoy with their self-righteous confidence. Job's real problem is with the Almighty. He cannot understand why God would let it happen. In fact, it looks to him as if God is responsible for his misery (16:7-17). Only a divine enmity is adequate explanation of so great calamity. Like some Hound of Heaven whose purpose is malevolent, rather than benevolent, God has relentlessly pursued Job: "worn me out" (v. 7); "shriveled me up" (v. 8); "torn me in his wrath, and hated me" (v. 9). Because of God's rejection, men also have made him the object of scorn (vv. 10-11). He was getting along fine when God snatched him up by the neck and shattered him on the ground (v. 12). Indeed, Job feels that he is being used for target practice. The cosmic arrows of an outrageous fortune are finding him, and he stands helplessly exposed like a defenseless man before his attacker, like a hapless city whose walls are breached again and again by an enemy (vv. 13-14). And this despite his mourning (sackcloth) and weeping and peaceableness and unselfishness in prayer (vv. 16-17). One without understanding of Job's rebellious grief may never have really sorrowed deeply.

Feeling that he is an innocent, helpless victim totally overmatched, Job has no hope of justice in this world. "The grave is ready for me," he says (17:1). But he cannot endure the thought that the case will simply be closed with his name still under suspicion. So he prays that his blood not be covered by the earth (see Gen. 4:10) nor his cry cease to echo about the world (16:18). His only hope is for "my witness in heaven" (16:19).

Who is this one who will "plead for a man with God, as a man pleadeth for his neighbor" (16:21, KJV)? He has already introduced the hope of a mediator (9:33) and will return to the theme again (19:25). His understanding of God includes little of love and grace. At this point he can only see God as an irresistible Cosmic Tyrant. But he is looking beyond himself to the necessity for an advocate. To be sure, he is still thinking of his own justification. He has not given up self-righteousness, but at least he knows that there is no hope of saving himself. So he can cry plaintively, "Who is there that will give surety for me?" (17:3). Who will go my bail until my trial may be arranged, then stand up before God on my behalf? Job's doctrine of God leaves something to be desired, but his growing realization of helplessness is putting him in God's reach. The rest of his speech alternates between rebuke of the counselors for their false accusations and announcements of his own imminent death.

Bildad's Second Speech: The Harshness of Self-Righteousness (18:1-21)

There is a rigid self-righteousness which is not only incapable of understanding the person who is different but is darkly pleased when "he gets what was coming to him." Such is Bildad's spirit. No new light appears in his second address. The attack on Job is merely heightened, employing the same argument already used, that the fate of the wicked is destruction. Implicit is the conclusion that Job must be wicked, else how explain his situation? Bildad begins sarcastically: Why do you talk to us as if we were stupid (v. 3)? You are the one who is so angry that you are practically tearing your skin off (v. 4a). (Is Bildad making thinly-veiled reference to Job's miserable skin condition?) Do you want the world overturned just because you are upset? (v. 4b).

Then he goes on to describe the fate of the wicked. His light, symbol of all good, will be put out (vv. 5-6). He will be tripped up by his own schemes (v. 7), trapped by his own evil devices (vv. 8-10), and terrified by bad conscience (v. 11). The reference in verse 13 to diseased skin must be a direct insult. But the worst thing Bildad says is saved until last. In verses

14-21 he argues that the wicked's ultimate punishment is not to have any heirs to survive him. His possessions will pass to strangers (v. 15). To leave no male heir was the worst of calamities, for a man's life was perpetuated through his name. But the wicked will be a tree with no branches (v. 16), leaving no name (v. 17), no survivor (v. 19). His fate will be a lesson to all men—west and east (vv. 20-21).

Job's Reply: "I Know That My Redeemer Lives" (19:1-29)

The reply of Job to Bildad's inference that he is getting what he deserves is closely akin to his earlier reply to Eliphaz (Job 16-17). Here as there he begins by denouncing his counselors (19:1-5), then says that God is responsible for his condition (vv. 6-22). Then he appeals to some future occasion when he believes that he will be defended and declared just through the good offices of a Redeemer (vv. 23-29).

Job's bitterness toward his comforters is plain in the opening lines of this reply. They "break me in pieces with words" (19:2). They won't let up on him—"ten times have ye reproached me" (v. 3). Moreover, although he admits no error, even if he has made one it is his own business and not theirs (v. 4). What they are doing is building themselves up by tearing him down (v. 5a). Ah, do we not know masters at that trade? Worse, they are taking a traditional dogma—that sin brings retribution—and arguing backwards from Job's "humiliation" to the conclusion that he must be a sinner or he would not be suffering (v. 5b).

Well, says Job, if you really want to know who is to be blamed for my condition, it is God (v. 6)! Here Job has gone about as far as he can reach toward blasphemy. Now God is the enemy. Like a helpless victim of a murderer's assault, Job screams, "Violence!" but nobody comes to his rescue because nobody wants to get involved (v. 7). So God the ruthless one continues the attack, penning him up so he cannot escape (v. 8), stripping him (v. 9) and breaking him down (v. 10) and treating him like an enemy (vv. 11-12).

Then Job describes vividly the loneliness of a man who is bereft

of any human compassion and support. Countrymen, acquaint-
ances, kinsfolk, close friends, servants, wife, brothers—all have
been turned against him, and God is responsible (vv. 13-20). It
is another example of how totally isolated Job feels in his anguish.
He believes that the whole creation is now estranged. What is
more, he blames God. Every pastor has sought to counsel and
comfort people who felt this total alienation. It brings suffering
which only the grace of God can assuage. Job's feelings are
irrational, but we should never suppose that they are unreal. He
concludes the description of his suffering with a last desperate plea
to the friends to understand. "Have pity on me! Can't you
understand?" (vv. 21-22).

Job has no hope of getting the matter settled and his name
cleared in this life. But some day the truth will come out! If
his words could be recorded, chiseled into rock with an iron stylus
using lead alloy for ink so that they might never be eradicated,
then his soul could rest, for he is confident of the eventual triumph
of justice (vv. 23-24). This brings Job to that sublime hope:
"I know that my Redeemer lives" (v. 25).

Few passages in the book of Job or in the entire Bible are
better known, but its interpretations have varied greatly, partly
because the Hebrew text of the passage (vv. 25-29) is not clear
and partly because of the diversity of views about the identity
of the Redeemer. The redeemer (*go-el*, Hebrew) in the Old
Testament is more than an avenger of the blood of a slain
relative (2 Sam. 14:11). He may be a next of kin who has first
option on the dead man's property to keep it from going out of
the family, or he may have the responsibility of marrying his
widow to bring up posterity to him. He may be in general a
defender of the helpless. He may be God the protector of his
people, or even of a single just person.

Who is the *go-el* referred to by Job? It is unlikely that Job was
thinking of a human being, for his children are all dead, his other
relatives and friends have deserted him, and besides, it is "at
last" (v. 25) and "after my skin has been thus destroyed" (v. 26)
that he looks for this vindicator. It is not God himself, for he

believes that God is his accuser, and it is through the agency of the *go-el* that he believes he will at last see God (v. 26). Yes, he will see God "in my flesh" (v. 26), "mine eyes shall behold" (v. 27) him. Is Job talking about some expected encounter with God while he is yet alive? We do not think so. We believe that Job is voicing the hope of an after life, in which his person would continue to exist and make it possible for him—through the Redeemer—to meet God face to face. The Redeemer of 19:25 is the Mediator of 9:33 and the Advocate of 16:19.

If this interpretation is correct, Job is a landmark in Hebrew thought about life after death. He is not prepared to make a definitive statement about the resurrection of the body, but he longs to see God. That has become a consuming passion. He believes that he will do so—not as a disembodied spirit, but as his total self. And the Redeemer will stand with him before the Almighty. Job's Redeemer is ours—Jesus Christ.

Zophar's Second Speech: Doom of the Wicked (20:1-29)

Little need be said about Zophar's second effort, for he only embroiders the tiresome theme of his predecessors: the doom of the wicked is sure. Here is a classic statement of the retribution doctrine. It recognizes that the wicked do indeed prosper, but answers that theirs is only a temporary respite from punishment. Zophar's certainly stems from tradition. "Do you not know this from old?" (20:4) he asks. "The exulting of the wicked is short" (v. 5) is the theme. It is like eating a rich meal which delights the taste but then turns sour in the stomach and must be vomited up (vv. 12-15). The inevitability of punishment catching up with the wicked is described in another figure as a man dodging an iron weapon only to be pierced by a bronze arrow (v. 24). Zophar is positive: "This is the wicked man's portion from God" (v. 29).

The argument has now taken this course: The law of reward and retribution dictates that you get what you deserve in this life. But, says Job, look around you and you will see innocent people suffering and wicked people prospering. Very well, reply the three friends, but this is only temporary. Before the end of their days the wicked will find the law of retribution has caught up with them. That sets the stage for Job to make yet another claim, found in his reply to Zophar's second speech.

Job's Reply: The Injustice of This Life (21:1-34)

As the second round closes Job is desperate. He pleads with his accusers to hear him carefully, after which they are free to mock him again if they wish (21:2-3). Have they no understanding of his impatience? Are they not appalled at the sight of him (v. 5)? He shudders when he thinks about it (v. 6).

Then he launches into a vigorous denial of the doctrine of earthly "evening up." A vivid picture of the life of the prosperous sheik follows (vv. 7-13). They reach old age, are mighty and wealthy, their children established and well off also. No calamity upsets their peaceful, well-to-do manner of living. God's rod strikes them not (v. 9); they come in peace to their death. More, these evildoers are also blasphemers (vv. 14-16). They say: Who needs God? What good does it do to pray to him? How often does it happen, Job asks, that such arrogance is punished with calamity? (vv. 17-18).

Well, you say, perhaps the wicked do not suffer calamity, but "God stores up their iniquity for their sons" (v. 19). Come now, replies Job, what kind of God will take it out on an innocent child? Don't ask me to believe in this kind of God (vv. 19-22). The fact is, Job continues, that death comes alike to all—the prosperous and the bitterly poor lying down alike in the dust (vv. 23-26). They should look at the evidence and ask people who have been around, who travel. Those with wide experience in life will confirm Job's judgment (vv. 27-31). Because of their wealth the rich are borne with great pomp to their graves (vv. 32-33). Job closes the second cycle with denunciation of his counselors and a rejection of their arguments as "empty nothings" (v. 34).

CHAPTER 5
Job the Defiant: When Hope Is Gone

The Third Cycle of Dialogue (22:1 to 31:40)

Eliphaz's Third Speech (22:1-30)

The three friends sense the failure of their mission. They had advised the sufferer to call upon God for forgiveness, but he had adamantly refused to admit guilt. Now they mount a final offensive. Eliphaz, as before, attacks first. Job has contended that God owes him an explanation, for he is suffering though righteous. They have held that Job cannot be righteous because he is suffering. But now Eliphaz would deliver God from involvement with man by pointing out that God has no need of him in the first place (22:2). We do God no favor by being good, but we do ourselves a favor. God has no lack which we meet, but we have many lacks. We cannot deny that God is complete without us (v. 3). But, of course, his argument is a half-truth, for it ignores God's great love for us.

But, says Eliphaz, we need all the help he can give us and when we sin he reproves us for it (v. 4). Inasmuch as God reproves sin, Eliphaz argues, Job must be one great sinner, since his suffering is so severe (v. 5). He then suggests an outlandish list of offenses which Eliphaz imagines must be so to account with justice for the severity of Job's suffering (vv. 6-11). Worst of all, says Eliphaz, is Job's blasphemous assertion that God is so far removed "way off there" among the stars that he doesn't see what is going on (vv. 12-14). Job had made no such claim about his own case. He had said that the wicked make a farce of religion and scoff at the notion that God is watching their nefarious behavior (21:14-16). Job has indeed accepted the idea of God's transcendence, but he has never said what Eliphaz accuses him of saying, "What does God know?" (v. 13). Job's frustration comes from believing that God does know, and because he knows he should correct the situation.

The closing section of Eliphaz's third discourse is another call to Job to repent (vv. 21-30). "If you return to the Almighty and humble yourself, if you remove unrighteousness far from your tents, . . . then you will delight yourself in the Almighty. . . . For God abases the proud, but he saves the lowly" (vv. 23, 26, 29). Eliphaz has learned nothing from the impassioned pleas of his friend. He still looks upon him as one who has done some awful wrong and who needs to repent and get right with God. That is the only sense that Eliphaz can make of Job's suffering.

Job's Reply: When God Absents Himself (23:1 to 24:25)

Perhaps it was Eliphaz's lofty theological statement about the transcendence of God, or perhaps it was his heartless closing appeal to Job to repent, but in his reply Job reflects an advanced stage of his helplessness. His feelings about God are more resigned. Once he had thought of God as his enemy. In the first cycle he had compared him to a hunter (6:4; 10:16), a terrifier of men (7:14-15), an irresistible snatcher of lives (9:12), and a killer (13:15). During the second cycle he continued such bitter denunciations: God is using him for cosmic target practice (16:12); God is like a ruthless warrior pillaging a defenseless city (v. 14); God has unjustly wronged him and cornered him like an animal caught in a hunter's net (19:6). But in the third cycle Job reflects the quiet mood of hopelessness and despair. He now thinks that there is total separation between him and God. Once he could resist, because he believed that God had feelings. Now he believes that his cries are met, not with divine wrath, but with divine indifference.

Once he had felt that God paid him too close attention and asked God to let him alone (7:17-21; 9:18; 10:16,20). He had hoped one day to renew fellowship with God (14:15).

Once he had been able to speak to God in prayer. In the first cycle he prayed five times, in the second only once (17:3-4), but in the last cycle he prays not at all. The loneliness of separation from God has descended like a cold chill upon his heart. This experience of God's absence is genuine in Scripture. Anyone who speaks too confidently about being in the center of God's will needs to look at his position in the light of the Bible. From the psalmists (see Pss. 22,42) to our Lord's cry of dereliction on the cross, there is an authentic note in the experience of God's people which is expressed in the words: "Verily, thou art a God that hidest thyself" (Isa. 45:15, KJV).

Job begins his reply to Eliphaz with one of the most eloquent statements in the Bible about man's search for God (23:1-9). Earlier he had longed for a Mediator (9:33), or an Advocate (16:19), or a Redeemer (19:25), but now he has no hope of anyone championing his cause, so he would like to plead his case personally to God. He wants an audience not as a humble, penitent, trusting servant but as one who would demand his rights. Whenever we seek God in such a mood we are sure to fail in the search. Job is not in a mood to ask God for help or guidance; he wants to "tell him off." He is convinced that such a confrontation would end in his own vindication (23:7).

What makes matters more intolerable in Job's eyes is that God appears to enjoy a little game of hide-and-seek with him. He knows where Job is and how Job has lived, and therefore God is being elusive. But it wouldn't really matter anyway, Job concludes, for God appears already to have judged Job guilty and is not about to be persuaded to change his mind. So Job feels that his situation is hopeless (vv. 10-17).

The first twelve verses of chapter 24 comprise a bitter tirade against God for his presumed indifference to human life. The wicked do all sorts of terrible things to the innocent and the righteous suffer all manner of indignity and injustice. The devastating conclusion of Job is, "Yet God pays no attention to their prayer" (24:12). How can Job pray to a God who he thinks does not hear prayers? The murderer, the adulterer, and the robber slip out under the cover of darkness to conceal their iniquitous deeds and are confident that they need not worry about God seeing (vv. 13-17).

In verses 18-20 and 24 there is a textual problem which the Revised Standard Version has sought to resolve by inserting the introductory words, "You say," before verse 18. The problem is that verses 18-20 and 24 do not express Job's view, but those of his three counselors. Job is contending in this passage that the wicked "get away with murder." Verses 18-20 and 24 argue, "But that is only temporary; soon the wicked are cut off," an argument which sounds more like Bildad or Zophar than Job. Some scholars believe that we have a displacement in the text here, inasmuch as Bildad's third speech is very brief and Zophar does not speak at all. Whatever disposition is made of the verses it should be clear that Job does not support the doctrine of delayed but certain retribution to the wicked in this life. That was the argument of the three friends.

Bildad's Third Speech (25:1-6; [26:5-14?])

In the present Hebrew text the third discourse of Bildad is composed of only six verses making up a brief doxology on the majesty of God, by contrast with which no man is good. Job's reply to these six verses is in its present order five chapters long, broken up only by the insertion at the beginning of chapters 27 and 29 (KJV) of the words, "Moreover Job continued his parable. . . ." Now, it is not the brevity of Bildad's words, nor the absence of any words from Zophar, nor even the length of Job's words, which poses any serious problem about the text of the five chapters. It is rather that chapters 26 and 27 contain material contradictory to Job's position but consistent with the views of the friends, and should therefore be assigned to them. Interpreters of the book of Job have generally recognized the problem, and while there is no unanimity of view, the following reconstruction of the text is frequently made, and is adopted by this writer: Bildad's third discourse, 25:1-6; 26:5-14; Job's third reply to Bildad, 26:1-4; 27:1-6, (11), 12; Zophar's third discourse (missing in the present text), 27:7-10, (11), 12-23; Job's closing discourse, 28:1 to 31:40.

In chapter 25 Bildad contrasts the indescribable glory of God (by whose luster the moon is dim and the stars are not clean, v. 5) with the condition of man. How can mere man claim to be righteous before God? Then in 26:5-14 the same thought is continued. God is irresistible. The ancient belief was that the region of Sheol was beneath the seas and the earth, and the deepest part of this nether region was called "Abaddon" (KJV, "destruction"). Nothing, even the darkest pit, is hidden from his omniscient eye. This is an eloquent poetic description of the power and majesty of God. It is not inconsistent with Job's thoughts about God, but it appears to many interpreters to complete the thought of Bildad in 25:1-6, while interrupting the thought of Job in 26:1-4; 27:1-6, (11), 12. Verse 14 is a beautiful metaphor of God's transcendent holiness: "How small a whisper do we hear of him!" (26:14). It is easy to claim too great a knowledge of God. How grateful we are that though we could not penetrate his divine otherness with our human reason, he broke into our humanity in his Son, Jesus Christ, to reveal himself to us!

Job's Reply to Bildad (26:1-4; 27:1-6, [11], 12)

The opening words of Job's final reply to Bildad are dripping with irony. What he says is that his three counselors have thoroughly misunderstood him. They have taken him for a man without wisdom (26:3). Even if he had been, their efforts would have been futile, for they had reflected such a bad attitude toward him that he cannot resist inquiring as to their inspiration. "Whose spirit has come forth from you?" (v. 4).

As Job again takes up his defense in 27:1-6 he utters a grim, determined oath of his innocence. By the very God who has "taken away my right" and "made my soul bitter" (v. 2), he swears to his integrity. As long as there is breath in his body, he will not let his lips be used for falsehood or his tongue as an instrument of deceit. He will tell the world that his heart does not reproach him for anything he has ever done (v. 6)! There are no fewer than twelve first personal pronouns in this brief statement, indicating Job's feeling of being deserted by God and his friends, and being driven back upon his own resources. He is the cornered, battered but still belligerent giant of a man who refuses to go down under the enemy's blows.

The remainder of this chapter, except for verses 11 (probably) and 12, does not reflect Job's position concerning God. The ideas sound like the arguments of the friends. As noted above, interpreters have pointed out this difficulty with the text as it stands, suggesting various rearrangements of it. This writer accepts the assignments made by Driver and Gray's important commentary on Job in the "International Critical Commentary Series." Verses 7-10 announce God's judgment against the unrighteous. Job's complaint had been just the opposite, that God did not cut off the godless.

The section comprising verses 13-23 speaks of the temporary success of the wicked. If anything good happens to them it is only to set them up for some greater calamity, like a man being blessed with many children only to see them killed, which would hurt him worse than never having had them. For Job to say such a thing would be inconceivable. He surely did not believe that his children had been killed because of his own sinfulness. God's favor upon a wicked man, says this section, is as ephemeral as a spider's web (v. 18), as insecure as a lean-to thrown up by a watchman to protect him from the weather (vv. 16-19). Job would not be likely to use such arguments, for they directly contradict the position to which he holds as he steadfastly maintains his innocence to the last (see 27:5-6). The verses do sound like the friends and, inasmuch as the text in its present form does not have a third discourse from Zophar, the passages discussed here (vv. 7-10, possibly 11, and 13-23) are frequently assigned to this third counselor. Of course, this is conjecture. We can let the text stand as it now reads but we put Job in the position of making statements which he has been protesting against throughout the book. It seems reasonable, in view of the above, to suppose that in the long course of copying the name of Zophar was lost out of this place in the text.

A Poem on Wisdom (28:1-28)

This "hymn to Wisdom" immediately follows the conclusion of the friends' attempts to break Job down to confess moral wrong-doing, and immediately precedes a closing soliloquy contrasting how it used to be with him and how it is, and concluding with a recitation of his virtues. It is a beautiful poem, teaching that wisdom is not a human attainment, but God's gift. Some inter-preters believe that the Hymn on Wisdom is either misplaced in the text or else was inserted after Job was written. Whether the poem is in its original place in the text we can not decide. But, much as 1 Corinthians 13, it is a self-contained literary gem with a beauty all its own and a truth forever valid: "The fear of the Lord, that is wisdom" (28:28).

The origins of Wisdom were briefly traced in the first chapter of this book. There it was seen that Wisdom, originally thought of as practical skill, came to be regarded as pragmatic piety, the "way to live." But it was noted that Wisdom had another mean-ing: the supernatural, transcendent mind of God. Some Wisdom writers personified it, as if it had a distinct and separate existence (see Prov. 8). Often it was spoken of as the means through which God acted as Creator, in this sense being close to the Fourth Gospel's teaching concerning the Logos (John 1:3). How does man acquire the "Mind of God?" The Hymn on Wisdom in Job 28 replies that it is through "fear of the Lord" and "to depart from evil."

The poem has three parts. Part One, verses 1-13, praises the technological skill of man, only to conclude that Wisdom is not to be found through man's cleverness. It is a difficult lesson for modern man, terribly impressed by what he can do. He mines silver and gold (v. 1), iron and copper (v. 2), digging deep into the heart of the earth (vv. 4-6), using light to make such underground exploration possible (v. 3). He channels the rivers, dams the streams (vv. 10-11). But in none of this magnificent human achievement is the source of true wisdom.

The next section of the poem dramatizes the worth of wisdom (vv. 14-22). It is worth more than gold or precious stones. The topaz of Ethiopia (v. 19) cannot compare with it. Whence comes wisdom (repeating the question of v. 12)? The answer (vv. 20-22) is that it is hid from the eyes of all living beings, that even the depths of Sheol do not know it except by rumor. The final section (vv. 23-28) affirms that only God has this secret. God is sovereign; he is in charge. He has set up the world and put everything in its proper place. God is the author and the dispenser of wisdom. It is not man's place to instruct God to give him wisdom. Instead, God says to man: "Reverence me and depart from evil doing—that is true wisdom."

Job's Final Soliloquy (29:1 to 31:40)

The argument with the friends is ended. Job's head is bloody but unbowed. In fact, if anything, he is more adamant than at the beginning. His final words before the Voice addresses him from the whirlwind are eloquent and plain, emphasizing that Job is derelict and alone. First, he reviews how it was in his salad days (29:1-25). Second, he tells how it is now for him (30:1-31). Finally, he recounts his virtues as a loyal son of Abraham (31:1-40).

First he talks about "the good old days." Ah, it was good then: "God watched over me" (29:2); I was in my creative years (v. 4); "my children were about me"—a pathetic cry (v. 5); and I was prosperous (v. 6). Moreover, he enjoyed the esteem of his community (vv. 7-13). When he went out to public meeting places such as the city gates or the square (v. 7), men young and old paid him deference (vv. 8-10). People everywhere blessed his name because of his generosity to the poor and needy (vv. 11-13). His good deeds merited the respect of his neighbors (vv. 14-17). He was eyes to the blind, feet to the lame, father to the poor. So he thought he would live his life out in peace, being blessed with many heirs to carry on his name (vv. 18-20). In fact, he was a leader of men in every sense (vv. 21-25).

But now look at me, he says in chapter 30, and you will see

the most incredible turn of events. He has become the object of scorn, even to the scum of the earth (vv. 1-15). Men younger than he (young men should defer to their elders), whose fathers Job would have disdained to hire as shepherds for his flocks, make sport of him! Here with unrestrained indignation he rages against this worthless, senseless, disreputable brood (v. 8) that in his former days would have been "driven out from among men" (v. 5). Now even this motley, ragtag crowd regards Job with scorn. He is a byword even to such a lot, who "do not hesitate to spit at the sight of me" (v. 10). And why do they dare to take such liberties? "Because God has loosed my cord and humbled me," he answers (v. 11). It is more than Job can bear and he cries out in effect: "I've had enough, more than enough!"

But as if the scorn of men were not more than he could bear, he has the awful sense of being rejected by God (vv. 16-23). God has cast him into the mire (v. 19). He cries to God and "thou dost not hear me" (v. 20, KJV). God tosses him about like a leaf in a storm (v. 22), and he is resigned to death and "to the house appointed for all living" (v. 23). The pathos of this chapter must reach the most indifferent heart. Job knows what it is to feel utterly alone. He is at life's darkest hour, and concludes with a cry of dereliction (vv. 24-31). Doesn't anybody understand? he begs. Isn't it normal for one in disaster to cry for help (v. 24)? When things were well with him he always tried to help those in need. But now when he looks for good only evil comes, darkness rather than light. The music of his life, once attuned to mirth, now knows only the somber song of mourning. There is nothing to look forward to except death and the grave.

Nevertheless, Job still asserts his innocence and so concludes with the most detailed account of his manner of life yet given. He does this by taking sixteen concrete situations where a man might transgress God's law (31:5-39). Each one is introduced by the conjunction "if," after which Job says in effect: "I am innocent." It is certainly the highest moral record to be found in the Old Testament. And he comes to the conclusion of it with the same grim determination with which he began the encounter, namely, that he is innocent of any wrongdoing.

The recitation of his virtues opens with the statement that he had "made a covenant with mine eyes" (v. 1, KJV) to live uprightly because he believed that God would watch over him and "count all my steps" (v. 4, KJV). So he has been truthful, honest, sexually virtuous, fair, generous, not greedy or proud, not an idolater, not envious or vengeful, hospitable, not hypocritical, not an abuser of the soil, and not one who ignores the tithe. It is a magnificent statement of human goodness, a veritable treasure-house of virtue.

Space limitations do not permit the examination of each of these sixteen statements of Job's case for nobility, but verses 13-16 may serve to illustrate the moral and ethical grandeur here. Job says that he has never mistreated a servant. The reason? Because the same God who made Job, wealthy community leader, also made that humble slave. If Job were to mistreat one of God's people, even though he be only a slave, "What then shall I do when God rises up? When he makes inquiry, what shall I answer him?" It is a remarkable statement, and one worthy of the Christian's most thoughtful consideration.

"The words of Job are ended," this chapter concludes. His case has been presented. What has he said at the end that he did not say at the beginning? Nothing, really, except to emphasize his innocence with specifics. The accusations of the three friends are ended, too. What had they accomplished? Nothing, really, except to deepen Job's feeling of desolation and alienation and to drive him to greater extremities. They attacked him with a great many words, the sum and substance of which was that he was bound to be guilty of sin, else he would not be suffering. Job was a sinner all right, as he was about to discover, but his sin was not such as they thought.

CHAPTER 6
An Angry Young Man

Near the end of his final speech Job had cried out to the Almighty to answer him (31:35). Reply comes from an unexpected quarter, a young man named Elihu, previously unmentioned and not mentioned again after his speech. Many commentators believe that the end of Job's words was originally followed immediately by the voice of Yahweh as reported in chapters 38-42. Reasons given are not only that Elihu nowhere else appears but also that in language and style the Elihu section (32:1 to 37:24) is noticeably different from the rest of the poem.

Be that as it may, we do not agree with critics who say that Elihu serves no purpose. His speeches are a preparation for the Voice from the whirlwind. Elihu denies the position of both Job and the friends. Job contended that his suffering is senseless and unjust. They held that it is the retribution of divine justice for sin. Elihu goes beyond both to argue that no matter what happens to him, man cannot deny the righteousness of God, and that suffering properly used may turn out to man's good.

Five prose verses in chapter 32 introduce Elihu, explaining who he was, why he spoke, and why he had waited until this occasion to speak. He is angry, so angry that he is "ready to burst" (v. 19), because Job had "justified himself rather than God" (v. 2). No less is he "angry at Job's three friends because they had found no answer, although they had declared Job to be in the wrong" (v. 3).

A comic note relieves the heaviness of Elihu's accusations. He is young and brash, full of himself, and impatient with his elders, arrogant, belligerent, and self-assured. We know him well! He begins by paying brief deference to age, but rushes on to declare that wisdom is not a matter of a man's years but whether or not the Spirit of the Almighty is in him (vv. 6-10). But Elihu confidently announces that he has the Spirit. After scolding the three friends because they were unable to confute Job (vv. 11-14), Elihu describes his irresistible urge to have his say (vv. 15-22). He can wait no longer (v. 16); he is full of words (v. 18); he is so wrought up that his heart is like fermenting wine that has no vent (v. 19); he must speak "that I may find relief" (v. 20). This is the comic note, the impatience of this bombastic young man so disgusted with his elders. But what he says—as is often true of the young—is worth hearing.

Job's Arguments Answered (33:1 to 35:16)

As Elihu turns directly to speak to Job he first seeks to establish rapport (33:1-7). He assures him of his own sincerity (v. 3), reminds Job that they are both "formed from a piece of clay" (v. 6) and should therefore talk "man to man," and concludes by promising not to be too hard on him (v. 7). Having sought to disarm Job, he then reviews three arguments which he has heard the sufferer give: (1) Job claims to be innocent (vv. 8-9); (2) Job claims that God is unjust (vv. 10-11); (3) Job claims that God is silent (vv. 12-13).

Elihu will undertake to reply to these charges, taking them up in reverse order. First, as to Job's claim that God is silent, Elihu says that the Almighty speaks to man in several ways, and that if man hears and repents, as he appeals to Job to do, he is accepted (vv. 14-35). For one thing, God speaks to man in visions; God is the God of revelation (vv. 14-18). Also, God speaks to man through his pains (vv. 19-22). The discipline of pain may be a great teacher. By it God may indeed find us as he had not been able to reach us before. But it was incongruous that Elihu should be instructing Job on the uses of adversity.

The third way by which Elihu suggests that God communicates with man is through an intercessor (vv. 23-25). The implications of the intercessor intrigue us. Elihu, youthful though he was, seems to have realized more than the friends that man needs help to plead his cause before a righteous God. Such an one intercedes for him to say, "Deliver him, . . . I have found a ransom" (v. 24).

This insight concerning the relationship between God and man is consistent with the gospel. Man cannot get to God by himself. But having the way opened up for him by the mediator, he knows himself to be accepted, to have received grace. Then "he comes into his presence with joy" (v. 26). Further, he becomes a witness to the grace which redeemed him even though "I sinned, and perverted what was right" (v. 27). God extends this offer of forgiveness again and again (v. 29), and therefore Job is urged to heed the word that, far from remaining silent, God is pleading with him to accept the fact that he is accepted (vv. 31-33). Elihu has in this manner anticipated Job's experience with the Voice from the whirlwind.

In chapter 34 Elihu speaks both to Job and the friends, refuting Job's claim that God is unjust. First, with a note of sarcasm about the "three wise men" who claim to know but are unable to answer Job, he states the problem (vv. 1-9). The problem is that Job has sinned by denying the moral order. "It profits a man nothing," Job has declared, "that he should take delight in God" (v. 9). Such a thought is outrageous to Elihu, and he enters an impassioned defense of the Almighty, in whom there is no evil, caprice, or unfairness (vv. 10-20). It is impossible that God should do wrong (v. 10). He requites man exactly according to his deeds (v. 11), and we can't interpret his grace as favoritism (v. 19). Indeed, without God's constant support all life would be obliterated (vv. 14-15).

Not only is God just, he is also omniscient (vv. 21-28). Thus, no man should suppose that he is getting away with anything. God knows his life. But more, God owes man no explanation (vv. 29-35). Job has complained that God is silent. Well, is it not his prerogative to be so if he chooses (v. 29)? He does not need to arrange his affairs to suit man (v. 33). Finally, Elihu attacks Job directly as having added rebellion to his sin (vv. 36-37). Again Elihu comes close to the truth revealed by the Voice from the whirlwind. He correctly discerns Job's response to his suffering—rebellion and presumptuous pride.

In chapter 35 he examines Job's claim of innocence and rejects it. To begin with, Job asks an improper question: "How am I better off than if I had sinned?" (35:3). He had assumed rights and prerogatives with God (v. 1). But, Elihu argues, God is transcendently independent of man. He is not hurt by man's sin or helped by man's righteousness (vv. 6-7). Job (7:20) and Eliphaz (22:2-3) had already noted that, so here Elihu is only restating a partial truth. The statement offers a corrective to man-centered religion by reminding us of God's transcendence, but it must not be used to support an unbiblical doctrine of divine indifference to man. God by nature may be invulnerable, but he is not unconcerned, and therefore sin affects God because sin affects man. Elihu can say that "wickedness (or righteousness) concerns a man like yourself" (35:8), but there is no way to limit its effects to the human plane.

Elihu's argument is one-sided but not pointless. He is insisting that God is in no way under man's control. The corollary of this he now states (vv. 9-12): God is to be sought and praised for his own sake, not for what he can do for us. People cry for God's help when they want relief, but they don't bother to acknowledge God as the author of life, nor are they eager to receive the gift of "songs in the night" (v. 10). That is, we cry for relief but we do not want to sing the song of trust which can turn the night into day. Then Elihu gets personal: What is generally true about man's attempts to manipulate God to his own purposes is particularly true of Job (vv. 13-16).

On God's Behalf (36:1 to 37:24)

Having dealt with Job's contentions, young Elihu turns his thought to the mystery and majesty of God. He would divert Job from preoccupation with himself and turn his eyes toward God in worship. "I have yet something to say on God's behalf," he begins (36:2). It is a sound biblical procedure. Let a man lose himself in adoration of God and he will have less occasion for self-pity. To achieve that purpose with Job, Elihu first discusses the mystery of the disciplinary and purifying effects of suffering (vv. 5-15). The key to this section is verse 15: "He delivers the afflicted by their affliction, and opens their ear by adversity." To such confident assertions we can only say, "Sometimes, depending upon the uses made of adversity. But is it necessary to suppose that God is the author of adversity just because some are able to profit from it?"

Before turning to the subject of the majesty of God as revealed in nature, Elihu delivers a last threefold admonition to Job to desist from his accusation of God because the wicked appear not to suffer (vv. 16-27). First, he should beware lest his anger lead him into a more grievous sin, thus getting further away from redemption (vv. 18-19). The second warning is against Job's toying with the idea of inviting his own death (v. 20). The third warning is against Job's adding iniquity to his rebellion (v. 21). He is already a rebel; let him not also become an iniquitous person. Instead, let Job join the chorus which sings praise to God (vv. 22-26).

At this point Elihu launches into a song of the wonders of God as revealed in nature, and particularly in the seasons of autumn, winter, and summer. Autumn (vv. 27-33) is a time of storm with lightning, thunder, and rain. The rain is a necessary part of God's refreshment of the earth and, spiritually speaking, the storms of life are ways in which God mysteriously expresses his great love for us. Winter (37:1-13) is a time of wonder, with snow and ice and the stilling of man's work and animal activity. God displays his power in the natural order, but more than that, the wonders of God in nature are but a pale copy of the wonder of God in his dealings with man. Summer, when "garments are hot" (v. 17) and the skies are "hard as a molten mirror" (v. 18), tells us that "God is clothed with terrible majesty" (v. 22). Elihu then bows out with a final innuendo that God has been silent to Job's pleas because of Job's egotism, for

God will not deal with those "who are wise in their own conceit" (v. 24). Elihu leaves, having prepared Job for the Voice from the whirlwind. He has not made the friends' error of calling Job's suffering the consequence of sin. But he does accuse Job of false charges against God. On that matter the voice of Yahweh now speaks to Job.

CHAPTER 7
The Voice from the Whirlwind

Job had repeatedly asked for audience with God (9:3,14-20, 32-35; 13:22; 31:35-37), but he has wanted it for wrong—though altogether human—reasons. He has wanted to declare his innocence and to protest his suffering. He has demanded that God justify himself for causing or permitting what has happened. Job gets his wish—God speaks, but he does not say what Job thought he wanted to hear. God does not accuse him of ethical transgression, but neither does he explain Job's suffering. There is no justification either of Job or of God.

Further, God does not tell Job that he loves him. He says nothing about the divine nature that Job does not already know and has not already either alluded to or mentioned directly. Yet at the end Job is reassured and satisfied. How could it be that out of this recitation of the wisdom and power of God Job finds peace? It can only be that Job realizes that he must live with the mystery. He can not get all his questions answered. If God is God his wonder and majesty are beyond us, yet not utterly so, for Job finds the peace of one who knows that he is known and has been heard. The God who speaks from the whirlwind had been speaking all along through event and through relationship. And Job sees that his sin was the presumption that he understood God and had the right to declare what God ought to do.

The message of Job is that God is God and that if we are to serve him acceptably it must not be in order to escape affliction or to be given special benefit, but because he is God and is to be obeyed and honored. Some may find this a harsh and partial gospel, and it is, needing the forgiving voice of Hosea added to it, and most of all the voice of Christ. Job is not the entire story of God and man. Missing is the tenderness of the Good Shepherd who lays down his life for the sheep. But it is an important corrective to a persistent and mischievous error, namely, that God may be manipulated by our good deeds. We too easily forget the sobering words of our Lord: "When you have done all that is commanded you, say, 'We are unworthy servants; we have only done what was our duty' " (Luke 17:10).

The words of Yahweh to Job fall into two divisions, after each of which Job makes a brief response. In the first section, chapters 38-39, by means of a series of rhetorical questions God's wisdom in ordering the universe is illumined. To this demonstration Job makes the simple response that he now realizes that he had been talking when he should have been listening, and he will be silent (40:3-5). In the second section of Yahweh's address the divine power in the universe is illustrated (40:6 to 41:34), after which Job makes his full confession (42:1-6).

The opening lines of Yahweh's address to Job set the tempo of the encounter. Job wanted to summon God and ask him some questions, but now finds that the really important ones are those posed by God which he is now called upon to consider (38:1-3). "Like a man" (v. 3) he is challenged to stand his ground and make his case. But he is soon to realize that he has no case. First, by the device of rhetorical question, Job is invited to consider the magnitude of the creation in contrast to the brevity of his own existence (vv. 4-15). "Where wast thou when I laid the foundations of the earth?" (v. 4, KJV). In a poem of sublime beauty the majesty of the creation is unfolded. Who determined the measurements of the earth (v. 5)? Or laid its cornerstone (v. 6)? Or fixed the borders of the sea (vv. 8-11)? Or ordered the precise timetable of day and night (vv. 12-15), causing the dawn to lift the cover of darkness from the earth exposing the wicked like one shaking a cover from a bed (v. 13)? When the morning comes the face of the earth is changed as the sunlight strikes it, like a seal impressing wax (v. 14).

Other wonders of the natural order which Job might consider

as he challenges the way God runs the world are the mysteries of the sea, and of death, and of light and darkness (vv. 16-20). Job is chided about his presumption: "You surely know these things, you who have lived so long!" (see v. 21). Then there are mysteries that have to do with the weather—snow and hail, lightning, rain, dew and ice (vv. 22-30). Another area where Job has no knowledge concerns the origin of the constellations (vv. 31-33). Another is the flood of rain (vv. 34-38). Can Job "tilt the waterskins of the heavens?" (v. 37).

From this survey of the wonders of the creation of the earth, sky, stars, and the elements, Yahweh turns the examination of Job to questions about the marvels of the animal kingdom. What does he know of the secrets locked in the instinctive life of the lion (vv. 38-40) or the raven (v. 41)? Can he explain the reproductive processes of the mountain goat and the deer (39: 1-4), or the habits of the wild ass or the wild ox (vv. 5-12)? Can Job explain the behavior of the ostrich in caring for her young (vv. 13-18), this ludicrous bird which can outrun a horse and rider (v. 18)? Who gives power to the horse (vv. 19-25)? The series of vignettes on animal life closes with reference to the soaring hawk, and the distant eagle with his nest in the rocks of the mountain (vv. 26-30). The animals chosen for review have one element in common—they are wild, not under man's control nor intended for his use. Man is invited to remember that his control of the world is really quite limited.

The first section of Yahweh's speech to Job concludes with a challenge: Will Job continue his stubborn dispute with God (see New English Bible on 40:2-3)? The effect upon Job of this initial encounter is dramatic. Suddenly he is no longer bellicose. His view has been raised from an ego-centered understanding of life to a God-centered one. In the light of God's universe he sees himself in truer perspective. Therefore he says: "Behold, I am of small account" (40:4). Once he had been full of words, bursting with righteous indignation against an order which would allow such unmerited suffering. He does not understand his suffering any better than he did before. His questions have not been answered. But he sees himself as part of a larger canvas. His understanding of God is being altered. He is willing to wait and listen. That is why he says, "I lay my hand on my mouth" (v. 4). He is not ready to admit that he needs to repent, but he does say that though he has spoken freely before ("once . . . yea, twice"—v. 5, KJV) he will do so no more.

The second part of Yahweh's address to Job (40:6 to 41:34) is largely concerned with a description of the creation and life of two massive beasts of the deep, Behemoth, the hippopotamus, and Leviathan, the crocodile. The significance of these will be examined briefly, but before doing so we look at a most important passage (40:6-14), in which God renews the challenge issued at the beginning of his address to Job (38:3). Does Job intend to deny the righteousness of God to make himself look better (v. 8)? It is a familiar device used in the art of self-justification. Job's sin is not the violation of ethical tenets, but the presumption of setting himself up as a judge of God.

Job has taken it upon himself to say what God ought to do, so the Almighty says to him, "Very well, do you think you are capable of being God? Have you an arm like God, and a voice like God?" (see v. 9). Then Yahweh invites Job to come on up and "play God" and see if he could do better (vv. 10-13). He would no doubt set the world right in short order! He would knock down the proud and stomp the wicked into the ground. What a god Job would make! If Job is capable of being God then he doesn't need God's help. If he can save himself then God will acknowledge it (v. 14). The irony must have reached Job at the deepest level. Job had thought it proper to pass judgment, but he is invited to sit in God's place and realizes that life is not so simple as he had supposed.

The section on the two monsters, Behemoth (40:15-24) and Leviathan (41:1-34), are puzzling. The two monsters may be seen as a continuation of the earlier discussion (39:1-30) about God as Lord of animal nature. These two creatures are wilder and more powerful than the others. Behemoth has been identified with the hippopotamus, Leviathan with the crocodile. Both are strange to the desert and the mountains, but are native to lush tropical regions. They probably have a symbol significance in the description of God as Lord of the universe. They remind us of the mysterious and primordial powers of life. God is author of all things, these strange realities as well as those with which we are familiar.

Job's Repentance (42:1-6)

The words of the Lord are ended. He has not answered Job's questions about his suffering. He has shown Job his "Godness." And Job is ready to make confession. Earlier he had been able to say only that he would be silent (40:4-5). Now he goes all the way. First, he acknowledges God's right and power to be God (42:2). Second, he confesses in humility that he had spoken out of turn, making pronouncements he had no right to make (vv. 3-4). Verses 3*a* and 4 are almost exact quotations from the introductory words of Yahweh to Job in 38:2,3*b*. It is almost as if Yahweh's words had lingered in his mind and he is now prepared to respond to them. The third aspect of Job's confession is that he realizes the presence of God (42:5). In some ways this is the climactic verse of the book. All of Job's and his friends' academic discussion about God is revealed in its true light—it has been the knowledge of tradition, of the "hearing of the ear" (v. 5). But now he encounters the reality about which he had had only secondhand ideas. And this personal encounter, as it always does (compare Isa. 6:5), moves him to self-abhorrence and repentance "in dust and ashes," that is, in great sorrow. Why is Job sorry? It is not because of some breach of God's moral code of behavior, but for a much more serious reason. In his unrelieved suffering he had falsely accused God of unconcern and injustice. Now he knows how wrong he had been.

The Epilogue (42:7-17)

The restoration of Job in the brief prose Epilogue troubles many. The burden of the poem has been that Job must love and serve God simply because God deserves to be served, not because he promises to even up all discrepancies in this life. Both Job and the friends at the beginning had believed otherwise. Believing as they did, the friends could only suppose that Job was guilty of some moral fault. Knowing that he was not guilty of moral error, yet holding the same doctrine, Job could only conclude that God was unfair. What he had learned is that our relationship with God, like any good human relationship, may not be measured in terms of how much the other does for us. God is not to be had for a price.

What is the meaning of the Epilogue? Its meaning is that God always gives us more than life takes away, though not always the same things that have been taken away. How could anyone ever compensate Job for the loss of his children? Does any parent suggest that the birth of another child replaces the one which has been lost? Monstrous! No, we must not dissipate the message of Job with a nice homily at the end about how God made it all up to him. What happened to Job was the enlargement of his life, the enrichment of his spirit, the deepening of his compassion, the broadening of his sympathies, and the heightening of his trust.

Job was restored, as many a person since who has sat like him on the heap of despair and, like him, in humble acceptance has encountered the voice of God out of the whirlwinds of life. What Job received from the Lord's hand after this encounter could never again be considered "my just due," but a grace, an evidence of life's givenness. In a sense all honor and wealth and children were his, because none were his. His life was not his own. It had been bought with a price.

PART II
The Message of Job to the Man of Today

CHAPTER 8
Does It Pay to Serve God?

"**D**oes Job serve God for nothing?" challenges our faith. God is so gracious and we are so selfish that it is easy to slip into the habit of counting our blessings in worldly terms. Jesus, who plainly believed in rewards, warned against the trap of doing good in order to get. When one succumbs to that, relationships suffer. No genuine love ever comes out of the motivation that asks with Simon Peter, "Lo, we have left everything and followed you. What then shall we have?" (Matt. 19:27).

The devil's cynicism about Job's motive for serving God can not be ignored. It reflects a view of religion which continues to enjoy wide currency. This view holds that God, being just, must surely reward the righteous and punish the wicked, else there is no moral order. A man prosperous in life and goods must therefore be pleasing to the Almighty; on the other hand one experiencing hardship must have displeased God and is being denied rewards.

The most likely conclusion to such reasoning is to turn religion into a pious pragmatism. That is the issue upon which the book of Job hinges. If Job's motive for serving God is presumed to be the goods he enjoys as a payoff, what will he do when all those goods are snatched away? Would he go on loving and serving the Lord because he believed it to be right and fitting for him to do so, and because there was in him a God-given capacity to respond with love to the divine love?

Both Job and his friends assumed at the beginning the posture of conventional religion. Because he knew that he did not deserve what he was getting, Job was indignant that his "good-works religion" had failed. He had put his money in the slot, and instead of something sweet, something indescribably bitter had come out. He felt cheated and was outraged.

The friends, believing the same doctrine, were confident that he was guilty of some enormity. How else explain such suffering, except as punishment? If not that, then the world is askew and the moral order is overthrown, they reasoned.

So Job burned with the hot anger of a man whose rights have been violated. But then he learned that what he had taken for his rights were not rights at all. He had no claim on God. God made him no promise of a life free from mortal anguish in exchange for his loyal service. What kind of relationship is it that must be merchandised—so much of my goods for so much of your loyalty? What kind of grace is it that is had for a price? To be sure, love joyously gives, but love is unrequited if rewards are necessary to assure response. God is not apt to say, "Come, let me bribe you to love me." Job learned that love is not love if it asks, "What's in it for me?"

Job's discovery, sharpened to a razor's edge by the awful tragedy of his own experience, must be ours. A good point of entry into this learning experience is the realization of God's impartiality. He does not have favorites. As Jesus put it, "He makes his sun rise on the evil and on the good, and sends rain on the just and on the unjust" (Matt. 5:45). If you suppose that being good should be rewarded by cash in the drawer, or in being healthy, wealthy, and wise, then you are going to be disillusioned. In a way, Job's protest is incontestible. Serving God may not pay off any better than not serving him. Remember those Galileans whose blood Pilate had mingled with their sacrifices and those eighteen people upon whom the tower in Siloam fell (Luke 13:1-5), or the house with the hush of death in it down the street from you.

There is even a sense in which the lot of the righteous is not only merely the same as the unrighteous, but often actually less pleasant. The reason becomes evident when one considers the sensitivity of the man who loves God as contrasted with that of the man who loves only himself. The godly man will be aware of his moral failure and folly, while he who has never stood ashamed in the holy presence of the spotless Christ escapes many a bout with his conscience. The man who believes in God can understand what Job meant when he said at the conclusion of his encounter with God: "I despise myself, and repent in dust and ashes" (42:6). In the same way, a concert pianist may be dreadfully upset if he plays a piece poorly while to the untrained ear there is no problem at all.

The road of the righteous is also more difficult because he is sensitive in another area—concern for others. Every gain carries a corresponding risk, every privilege a corresponding responsibility. He who asks to be initiated into life's secrets has got also to prepare himself to carry its burdens.

Parents know that. Parenthood is a risky business—risk to the mother's health, risk that the child will not be sound of mind or body, risk of disease and accident, and risk that after all the sacrifices the child will turn out to be a useless, ungrateful wretch. The more one loves, the more one is exposed to hurt. The more lines of concern one sends to others, the more often will an alarm sound in the heart from one of those lines. God has paid us "the intolerable compliment" of letting us share the glory and anguish of loving.

But something more needs to be said about rewards. True, God does not want us hustling him for handouts, any more than a parent wants that sort of relationship with his child, but it is not true that there are no rewards. Although the Epilogue in Job must not be interpreted to say that Job was rewarded at the end because he had earned it, it is there to remind us that life has both consequences and unexpected bonuses. We cannot measure out life's returns by the pound, so much goodness producing so much blessing, but we had better not make the mistake of supposing that nothing we do or don't do matters.

There is a connection between what one does and the results of what one has done. Denying it would make life a senseless game of charades. There would be no difference between the effect of one act and that of its opposite if we reject the existence of rewards. That is to turn life into an absurdity. There is a direct relationship between the way we live and the things that happen to us. But that is a far different thing from contending that whatever happens is a reward or a retribution visited upon us by God. Job was a man who got something he did not deserve. We all do, both evil and good. Our lives are not only hurt by events we did not cause, but are also blessed by other happenings we did not produce.

Further, we are rewarded in the area in which we labor. That is the constant note of Jesus. He often spoke of rewards, holding that life tends to give us what we go after. Thus, in the Sermon on the Mount, he warned against preoccupation with seeking the praise of men. Such ambition could turn the religious acts of almsgiving, prayer, and fasting into vulgar self-displays. These would earn the praise of men, which was their purpose, but would not get the approval of God. Those who do such things "have their reward" (Matt. 6:3,5,16). Paul makes the same point in his letter to the Galatians: "Whatever a man sows, that he will also reap" (6:7). One doesn't sow spiritual seed and expect to reap a material harvest.

Does it pay to serve God? Yes, because the attractiveness of not doing so is a grand deception. Sometimes we envy the cheerful pagan. Look at him, we say, he does not seem to suffer a horrible fate. Who said he would? What has that got to do with it? You would not contend that stealing is an acceptable act so long as one is smart enough to avoid getting caught. No, stealing is morally wrong and unacceptable to a Christian even though he may never get caught. You cannot put doing right or wrong on the basis of reward and retribution. There is a higher claim.

We have overplayed the hand of sinfulness. Its price is great. What a man pays for his prejudice, anger, hatred, immorality, or greed is fearful. The psalmist puts the matter eloquently: "And he gave them their request; but sent leanness into their soul" (106:15, KJV). Many a man gets the desires of his heart and supposes that that is the end of it. But it isn't. He may be unaware, but he suffers "leanness of the soul." One thinks of Samson who "did not know that the Lord had left him" (Judg. 16:20). Poor simple Samson! He had fooled around with the delights of sin until he overplayed his hand.

Does it pay to serve God? Yes, because of judgment. Judgment is not simply some final, remote decision to be rendered. Judgment is also accumulation. Judgment is becoming. Every act, word, and thought turns me a little. I am becoming. Some day I shall be confronted with who I have become. Like buying on credit, it isn't the day when the bills come due that is my real undoing, but the folly of unrestrained credit buying. Judgment is the cumulative impact of an almost infinite number of individual decisions of character. When the Christian speaks of reward, he is thinking about what in Christ he is becoming. "And we all . . . are being changed into his likeness from one degree of glory to another" (2 Cor. 3:18).

Does it pay to serve God? To doubt it is to overlook the joy of doing right. It may well be that in our effort to state the claims of Christ seriously we have caricatured discipleship into an oppressive, deadly, and joyless affair. How different from that Jesus was! His buoyant joyousness was a scandal to many of the pious in his day. The discipline to which he summoned men was indeed a life-and-death engagement, but it was not a sad and dreary one. He promised not only a cross, but intoxicating joy. It would be like a man quite unexpectedly finding a treasure in a field and "in his joy he goes and sells all that he has and buys that field" (Matt. 13:44). Let not fear of loving God for the wrong motive—what we can get out of it—deprive us of the joy of freely loving him.

CHAPTER 9
"Who That Was Innocent Ever Perished?"

One bright sunny fall afternoon tragedy struck suddenly on the high school football practice field during the first real scrimmage of the fall. An ordinary line play left a boy lying at the bottom of a heap of players. He had a broken neck. Worse, his spinal cord was severed. He was a fine lad with great promise. In the hospital he said, "Pray for me." But in two weeks he died. Why? If someone were to blame it would be easier to understand. Poor coaching? Faulty equipment? Ill-conditioned players? "Dirty" football? None were factors in the moment of disaster which plunged an entire community into grief.

Of all the words in the language of man, none can be sharpened to a keener edge than the word "why." Why does God allow suffering? If he is almighty, could he not prevent it? And if he is good, why doesn't he? The poet, Archibald MacLeish, in his play written on the Job theme called *J. B.*, states the problem cryptically in words recited by the Satan character: "If God is God He is not good, if God is good He is not God."[1]

The universality of the problem only makes it more acute. Sooner or later, we all have occasion to ask, "Why?" In this sense, Job is everyone of us. Indeed, MacLeish puts the enormity of chance, innocent suffering in dramatic words:

> Millions and millions of mankind
> Burned, crushed, broken, mutilated,
> Slaughtered, and for what? For thinking!
> For walking round the world in the wrong
> Skin, the wrong-shaped noses, eyelids:

> Sleeping the wrong night wrong city. . .
> Job is everywhere we go,
> His children dead, his work for nothing. . .[2]

One of the oldest, easiest, most persistent, and most untenable answers to the question is a simple one of associating well-being with righteousness and trouble with evil. Since God is good and a rewarder of them that love and serve him, it would appear that "living right" would assure immunity from the common human condition. That it doesn't seems not to occur to a host of pious people until it happens to them. This was the view of Job's friends. That is why they could patronizingly call him to repentance. When Job protested his innocence, they gave him a knowing look and said: "Think now who that was innocent ever perished?" Ask that of Hiroshima, or Auschwitz, or knock on the next door you see with crape hanging on it. Whatever answer we give to this perplexing problem, we must never say simply, "God rewards the innocent and punishes the guilty."

As a matter of fact, there is no simple, airtight answer to the problem of innocent suffering, given faith in an all-powerful and all-loving God. But there are some things we can say. For one, it is the kind of world in which the suffering of the innocent is a necessary possibility. For example, it is a finite world. We are limited in many ways—by our ignorance, by other people, by the very order which holds the universe together and causes it to operate in a dependable way. All of these finite limitations may cause us to suffer innocently.

Moreover, man is given a great deal of freedom in this finite, orderly world. If God had not allowed us freedom to make wrong choices he might well prevent our ever getting hurt, like a parent overprotecting a child so that the child never learns to make decisions. Sometimes the parent has to risk the child suffering injury in order to allow him to exercise his freedom. Only in the exercise of freedom is growth possible.

Further, our very humanness is occasion for our suffering. It is man's great capacity to feel, to care both for himself and for others, which makes him vulnerable to pain. If he had the nervous system of an oyster he probably would not suffer greatly. But would he not also be deprived of his manhood? A world without pain would be an inhuman world.

These, then, seem to be the basic conditions of our humanity which make suffering inevitable. But this is not to say that suffering is God's will. Much that is attributed to providence is simply the inevitable result of man's folly or sin. Sometimes it is our own folly or sin. If we play the fool, we must not expect always to be spared the harvest of folly. God is no safety catch to keep the gun from going off.

Sometimes the sin and folly are not attributable to the sufferer, but he is the innocent victim of another's wrong. His suffering may, in fact, be all the more acute because he does not deserve it. But our lives are so interrelated that we do not confine consequences, good or bad, to ourselves. Can I blame God if some drunken driver hits my car and maims me for life?

Another source of human suffering comes from those mysterious and inexplicable disasters where no one appears to be at fault. Lightning strikes, a tornado sweeps down, a piece of machinery fails, disease attacks. To be sure, no situation involving persons is wholly devoid of the human factor, but multitudes of occasions occur where it is impossible to say, "If so-and-so had not done such and such this would not have happened." Many tragedies defy explanation. Shall we attribute these to God's will? But if we live in a universe of order, how can we require that we be exempted from its operation?

There is a fourth category of suffering. It is that which one takes voluntarily upon himself on behalf of others. This is vicarious suffering. The larger the vicarious element in an act of self-sacrifice, the more powerfully redemptive it is. So Christ, "who knew no sin," was made to be sin for us, "that we might be made the righteousness of God in him" (2 Cor. 5:21, KJV). Think, now, about the question, "Why do we suffer?" Do not these four categories cover all the cases you know? We bring it upon ourselves, or we inflict it upon others or they upon us, or we are the victims of events for which no cause is known, or we voluntarily accept suffering to give life or help to someone else.

We have seen that the kind of world we live in is one in which the possibility of suffering seems unavoidable. We have looked at the sources of man's suffering. Now let us consider God's role in human suffering. If he could prevent it, why doesn't he? Are we left between the choices of a God who is either impotent or indifferent?

We have to begin from the point that God could prevent suffering if he chose to do so. Ultimately, everything that happens is God's responsibility. You could not get hurt if God had not made it possible. Why didn't he? Without claiming to know more than we do or can, we can surmise at least two reasons. These have already been alluded to. One is that to surround us with protection so that we could not hurt ourselves or others would be to destroy us as persons. It would be much like locking a child up in a padded cell.

The other reason why God did not make life to be free from suffering is a bit more difficult to defend, but no less true. It is that we seem to need it. It adds a dimension to life without which we are incomplete. In fact, in one of the most startling verses in the Bible, the author of the letter to the Hebrews says of Jesus: "Although he was a Son, he learned obedience through what he suffered" (5:8). And later in the letter this writer encourages his readers who are suffering persecution to accept it as a sign that they are loved by God, for the persecution may be seen as God's discipline. "For the moment all discipline seems painful rather than pleasant: later it yields the peaceful fruit of righteousness to those who have been trained by it" (12:11). What is the old adage about "sparing the rod"?

This is a hazardous doctrine, used to make God responsible for all kinds of outrageous conditions. If plagues come from human filth, or fires from human carelessness, or floods from human abuse of God's soil, or wars from human hate and greed, shall we call these "acts of God"? Shall we make God responsible for cancer or crime? If so, do not all who labor to eradicate these evils work against the purpose of God? Nonetheless, we must never seek to reduce God's relationships with us to doling out sweetness and light. The plain fact is that we must prepare ourselves to face the problem, for suffering is a part of life. We do not have light without darkness, the glory of the morning without the stillness of the night. What is more, we learn some lessons through suffering and sorrow never before taught us.

Far more important, however, than speculation about why we suffer is letting God help us when we do. At this point, the apostle Paul's experience is illustrative. He knew a great deal about pain. That "thorn in the flesh" (2 Cor. 12:7) was a constant source of distress. No amount of praying brought relief. He had to put up with it, and God gave him grace to master it. The outcome was that the very weakness gave occasion for the demonstration of God's power. God had not delivered Paul from his trouble, but had delivered him in it.

His familiar words in Romans 8:28 state the Christian case clearly: "We know that in everything God works for good with those who love him, who are called according to his purpose." This inspired observation says simply that we have God's help in handling everything that happens. This is no promise of immunity from trouble. Indeed, the very passage contains a recitation of some of the perils to which we are daily exposed. But none of these things—though they happen—can separate us from the love of God which is in Christ Jesus our Lord.

Four of the good things God may accomplish in our suffering may now be noted. First, we may gain a better understanding of life. Suffering can be a great teacher. "I have learned more from three prolonged illnesses than I have ever been able to get from books," a prominent American minister told his congregation in a sermon preached the last year of his life. But there is nothing automatic about it, to be sure. Some people learn from suffering only new dimensions of their own bitter souls.

Second, suffering may bring an enlargement of our capacity to care for other people. It does not necessarily follow, however, because many respond to the hurting in themselves by becoming more selfish and self-centered. But in Christ, the man for others, we can know what it is to belong to "The Fellowship of those who bear the Mark of Pain," to use Albert Schweitzer's phrase. He describes the Fellowship thus:

Those who have learnt by experience what physical pain and bodily anguish mean, belong together all the world over; they are united by a secret bond. . . . He who has been delivered from pain must not think he is now free again, and at liberty to take life up just as it was before, entirely forgetful of the past. . . . He must help to bring to others the deliverance which he has himself enjoyed.[3]

Third, suffering may bring a strengthening of character. The wrinkles that crease a mother's face may be a roadmap of the journeys of care she has traveled, and each line speaks eloquently of character. Or to change the figure, suffering may be a refining fire that burns out the dross, purifying life's purposes.

Thornton Wilder, in a short play written on the theme of the Pool of Bethesda, illustrates the point. It is of a physician who bears a secret disability and who comes to the pool to be healed when the angel stirs the waters. But as he is about to plunge in the angel stops him: "Draw back, physician, . . . Healing is not for you. . . . Without your wound where would your power be? It is your very remorse that makes your low voice tremble into the hearts of men. The very angels themselves cannot persuade the wretched on earth as can one human being broken on the wheels of living. In Love's service only the wounded soldiers can serve." Another flings himself into the troubled water and is healed. The disappointed physician turns slowly away. As he does, one newly healed pleads with him: "Come with me . . . , an hour only, to my home. My son is lost in dark thoughts . . . Only you have ever lifted his mood. Only an hour . . . my daughter since her child has died, sits in the shadow. She will not listen to us. . . ."[1] There is a great truth here. Suffering may tap reserves of previously unused character.

Finally, suffering may deepen faith in God. It did that for Job. Before his suffering he knew God only "by the hearing of the ear." But through it he came to a firm personal faith in

God: "Now mine eye seeth thee." Suffering elicited the same response from Paul. Writing of a particularly perilous period in his life when he had despaired of surviving, he said: "Yet we believe now that we had this experience of coming to the end of our tether that we might learn to trust, not in ourselves, but in God who can raise the dead" (2 Cor. 1:9, Phillips). Paul's extremity had indeed become God's opportunity.

There is no guarantee that suffering, innocent or deserved, will produce such results as here suggested. Often its harvest is bitterness, self-pity, and despair. The difference is not in what life brings to us but in what we bring to life. Or to quote Paul again: "The pain God is allowed to guide ends in a saving repentance never to be regretted, whereas the world's pain ends in death" (2 Cor. 7:10, Moffatt).

CHAPTER 10
"Now Mine Eye Seeth Thee"

For most people the crucial religious issue is not belief in God's existence. This is not to suggest that there is no honest atheist. It is to say that some ultimate concern is so nearly universal among us as to make exceptions relatively rare.

The critical religious problem of every age is the absence of a sense of personal relationship with him. The ancient Greeks, for example, did not doubt the existence of the gods, but they avowed that the gods were not and, in fact, could not be concerned about man. They even had a word for the divine attitude toward man—*apatheia*—from which our word "apathy" comes. The reasoning behind such a view was that if you care about another, he affects you to the extent of your concern. The parent is not free of care if his child's welfare is in jeopardy. In a real sense, the parent is limited by the child. Mortals cannot limit the gods, the Greeks argued, but they would be limiting them if the gods cared for men.

From what is perhaps a more scientific standpoint, many a modern constructs his view of God along Greek lines. The universe is too vast, he says, for me to indulge in the fond hope that the Almighty may be aware of or concerned about me. Is it not the height of presumption to suppose that he has come to me as a Person to a person? In the words of a young woman in college far away from home, writing to her father: "Can God become a reality like people are or like a particular person?" This is the crux of our Christian faith. The gospel's answer is a resounding affirmation. The God of the universe who created the reality we know and who exists apart from it without removing himself from it, has entered our human life and made himself known in Jesus Christ. And he continues to make himself known through the Spirit of Christ, the Holy Spirit.

That is also one of the major concerns of the book of Job. How does a man who has all the orthodox beliefs about God but who does not know him personally come to encounter the Almighty, and what happens to him when he does? As this great and good man, Job, wrestled with the fundamental issue of knowing God he came to see that being formally religious, morally upright and doctrinally correct are not enough.

Job is a special kind of candidate for illustrating the way by which man comes to a personal knowledge of God. His flawless rectitude makes him an unparalled example that piety alone does not bring one into personal relationship with God. Had he been an average man, leading an ordinary life, moderately good and bad, it might have been argued that his sins stood between him and God. But the writer presents an extraordinary man, "blameless and upright, and one that feared God and turned away from evil." Not only is he personally moral, but also the epitome of parental godliness, frequently offering sacrifices on behalf of his children, lest in their youthful folly they be guilty of some unforgiven sin. Here is a rare specimen—a man whose practice matches his profession. Yet he is also the man who at the end of his experience confesses: "I had heard of thee by the hearing of the ear, but now mine eye seeth thee."

As the incredible list of disasters is recited, one wonders how much a mortal can endure. But there Job sits, broken in health but not in spirit, as fine an example of Stoic courage as you will ever see. His sense of his worth as a man holds him together. It is an awesome sight, this indomitable human spirit that refuses to give in to the indignities to which disease and disaster can subject the human frame.

There the story of Job might have ended save for his three "friends." They meant well. What a commentary on intentions! They misunderstood his need. They came to bring advice; he was in desperate need of companionship and comfort. They came with a sterile theology of reward and punishment; he was confronted by an awful reality. They kept telling him to repent of sin and trust in God, promising that everything would then be all right. But in his desperation he did not even know how to find God, much less trust him. What he needed was compassion. What he got was a series of stale, secondhand religious cliches and moral platitudes. They kept insisting that God punishes the evil and rewards the good. Once he had believed that himself, but now he saw that that doctrine did not cover all the facts. He was one of the facts it did not cover.

In his desperation Job cried, "Oh, that I knew where I might find him." That might have been the climactic moment of the story of Job except that at that point his reason for wanting to find God was not to confess his need of God but rather to justify himself before God. No man ever finds God when his purpose is to recommend himself to the Almighty.

Then the cold, stoical statue of the "correct" man began to crumble. Job sensed that he was coming apart, hammered by the blows of his accusers who represented the traditions of his people. He whimpered and complained, wishing that he might die or, better still, that he had never been born. Defiance followed complaint. God was attacking him without cause. He called God dreadful names: capricious tyrant, corrupt judge, wild beast, ruthless warrior. His physical pain and spiritual anxiety caused him to magnify his own person. In these wild ravings of a desperate soul he began to think only of himself. He imagined himself to be the cosmic victim of God's arrows shot into his helpless body.

The patient was as sick as he could get. Things had to go one way or the other. The man could not stand any more. What was to become of him? In his extremity for the first time he heard the voice of God! And the words God spoke to Job were not a mere repetition of the pious remarks already offered by the three friends. Nor were they the cajoling and begging pleas of a parent trying to induce a spoiled child to get up off the floor from a kicking, screaming tantrum. They were words of rebuke, of judgment, and of acceptance.

"Little man," God said to Job, "don't you think you are taking yourself too seriously, picturing yourself as a target for the whole universe? What do you mean accusing me of being unfair? Who are you to say what is ultimately fair and unfair? Where were you when I laid the foundations of the earth, unrolled the carpet of the universe, hung the stars in the sky, and commanded the sun to shine?" And Job began to see himself for the first time. The good, pious, moral man saw himself as the same man, who under sufficient stress, had not in himself the strength to maintain his fidelity. He saw himself and the outlandish, mawkish claims he had made that "life is against me." And most of all, he saw himself as in need. There was no sufficiency in him. His piety, his morality, his bravery—all were not enough.

Thus the divine-human encounter took place. Job, who had known about God, experienced him. "I had heard of thee by the hearing of the ear, but now mine eye seeth thee." Then the voice which once had hurled defiance against heaven and angrily pronounced its own innocence confessed humbly: "Therefore I despise myself, and repent in dust and ashes." That is the key to Job's experience. We are not helped much by the Revised Standard Version rendering, "I despise myself," any more than by the more familiar King James, "I abhor myself." Perhaps a truer understanding of Job's feelings would translate the words: "I melt into nothingness, I flow away." This is the authentic note. In the presence of God, the self retires. The man who encounters God is not overly impressed with his own merits.

It is significant that Job found God at the end of his rope. Do we ever find him anywhere else? He heard God's voice from out of the whirlwind. Do we ever really hear him so clearly as in the midst of storm? It is important to remember that God did not reassure Job of his innocence. Job was not innocent. True, he was not guilty of the moral error which the friends suspected, but he was guilty of worse sins. He had defied God, set himself up against God, presumed to tell God how to be God and run the universe. It was Job's presumption which God rebuked and of which Job repented.

See, now, where Job found God. He did not find him through the correctness of his beliefs about God, nor through personal piety. There is scarcely a harder lesson to learn, as the rich young ruler dramatically illustrates. Paul preached that man could not be saved by his good works, a risky kind of gospel that could be and was twisted into a frightful abandonment of morality. But despite such aberrations Paul continued to preach the gospel of justification by faith. Redemption by human effort means a return to the slavery of legalism and the killing pride that it engenders.

Job did not find God through the medium of his friends' words about God, ever so orthodox as they might have been. Perhaps if they had lectured less and loved more he might have found God through them. This is not to discount personal witness, but it is to say that we do not find God secondhand, any more than a boy learns the sea by listening to the yarns spun by a seasoned sailor. Each man must experience for himself.

Job did not find God through his sorrow. It was not a simple matter of hammering this proud man to his knees. The blows he suffered did not bring him to God. Through much of the experience he stoutly defended his sense of outrage at his fate. Sometimes a person is hardened and made bitter by tragedy. Sorrow of itself has no power to heal.

Job did not find God through proclamation either of his innocence or of his guilt. With the first—his innocence—one would anticipate little disagreement. But the mere declaration of his guilt would not bring the awareness of God's forgiveness and healing, either. Many a man uses the vulgar display of his unworthiness as only another means of calling attention to himself. "Look at me," he says with ill-concealed admiration of his own naughtiness. As long as I look at myself I will never see God.

Where did Job find God? He found him at the point of his dire need. He found God in his utter aloneness, with every vestige of support stripped away, especially a smug, self-satisfied doctrine of God. All that gone, Job stands alone, and in his aloneness he hears the voice of God.

We cannot say that the book of Job answers all of man's need concerning relationship with God. For instance, there is no note of God's love in the book. God does not reassure Job that he loves him at all. Such reassurance we know in Christ. What Job does learn is the limit of his own understanding. He cannot run the universe for God. He must accept his humanity and trust God to be God. He is not in a position to instruct God about righteousness. He now sees that his sin was a terrible presumption. Of this he repents, seeking forgiveness and restoration.

God does not answer all of Job's questions, yet he is satisfied, for in his dire need he has not been denied the presence of God. At the end he was no nearer than at the beginning to an understanding of the mystery of innocent suffering or the prosperity of the wicked. But answers to these mysteries could wait, for now he had been confronted by God himself. If a man knows that he is known, that he is not lost in a vast sea of uncaring impersonalness, that his name has been called and he has been addressed by the Lord of all, then he can bear not knowing all secrets and not having all answers. Like a rebellious, angry child, who feels ignored and by his naughtiness demands attention, Job had railed at God. But like that child, for whom even parental punishment may be a form of reassurance that the parent cares, Job learned that God did not ignore him. And in that knowledge he found comfort.

CHAPTER 11
Is That All There Is?

A recently popular song heard a year or two ago raised this question. A sultry-voiced songstress recounted several key events of life, such as growing up, falling in love, getting married. All were disappointing and unfulfilling. After each came a refrain that went something like this: "Is that all there is, my friend? Then keep on dancing. Break out the booze, let's have a ball, if that's all." The song concluded with a momentary speculation that the final great event might make up for all the previous letdowns. But the singer murmured, "Oh, no, I'm not ready yet for that last great disappointment."

The song is disturbing, perhaps intentionally so, because of its pathos. It can see no deep meaning or lasting joy in any earthly experience. The singer's thirst is unquenched by the best that life has to give. The spirit of the song is that of a spoiled child who, taken to Disneyland, looks around with casual boredom for a few minutes and then says wearily, "What else have you got to show me?"

But saddest of all is the suggestion that the great adventure of death will turn out to be just another big bust. Death is not even dreaded; it is merely delayed as the last of the succession of disappointments. It should not be embraced too readily. One might as well go on playing the game, dull as it is, for it is probably better than no game at all.

How different is the Bible in its attitude toward life! Like a fresh spring breeze blowing through a stale room, its word of hope sounded through the ancient world. Its pages are peopled with men and women alive to life's wonder and glory, and sensitive to its hurt. Job is no exception. In the intensity of his suffering, he never declared that God doesn't matter, or that life is meaningless. He did despair of his life. He railed against God. But he never turned life off as a dull affair. Indeed, it was at times a terrifying, nearly unbearable one. As to the possibility of life after death, Job wavered between hope that there might be, and the common belief of his contemporaries in Sheol, that "no-man's-land" where the dead resided in shadowy, meaningless unawareness. That uncertainty added to his agony.

Listen as he laments the brevity of his earthly life and what he sees to be its end: "My days go swifter than a weaver's shuttle, to reach a hopeless end. O God, my life is but a breath. . . . I will never thrive again. . . . As a cloud fades and disappears, so he who passes down to death rises no more; never shall he come home again, never shall his place know him any more" (7:6-7, 9-10, Moffatt). Or hear this plaintive cry of one wrestling with the issue of death: "Man born of woman lives but a few days and is full of trouble; he flowers and fades, he is a fleeting shadow. . . . There is hope for a tree that is felled; it may flourish yet again. . . . But man dies and departs, man breathes his last—and where is he? Like the water of a vanished lake, like a dry, drained river, man lies down, never to arise, never to waken, though the skies wear out, never to stir out of his slumber" (14:1-2,7, 10-12, Moffatt).

For the most part Job shared the accepted Hebrew view about death as the end of significant life. The remarkable thing is not that he believed in Sheol, where the dead existed meaninglessly, but that at moments his spirit rises on the wings of an exhilirating hope that a real life of communion with God might take place after death. Such a hope surfaces at the very point of the despair. Job's religion instructs him to accept Sheol, but his heart bursts forth in a plea for life.

Perhaps a period of waiting in Sheol would be necessary until God's wrath be past (14:13). After that, might there be an appointed time when God would remember him? Remember me! It is the plea of the penitent thief on the cross, and the cry of every man who dares to believe that he was not born to be forgotten by God. So Job raises the question which every man asks sooner or later: "If a man die, shall he live again?" (v. 14). That is a question we cannot let alone because death will not let us alone. It is not some egotistical desire to live on in uninterrupted bliss that prompts Job's question, and ours. It is the desire to know God and to have communion with him. So Job pictures it as if it were a return to Eden where God, longing for the work of his hands, would call and man would answer (v. 15). It would be a beautiful relationship in which God would not deal with man according to his sin, but according to his own divine mercy (vv. 16-17).

It is a glorious thought, but Job, like any person in grief, is pouring out his soul without reference to logical consistency. He has risen from the depths of despair to soar briefly at the dizzy height of hope for life after death. But immediately he falls back to earth again with the conclusion that death really is the end of man (vv. 20-22).

In another sublime moment Job breaks forth in hope for life after death. This is the familiar passage in which he proclaims: "For I know that my redeemer liveth" (19:25, KJV). The redeemer is not a human relative who in accordance with Hebrew custom will defend his honor, but one who is going to stand up for him at "the latter day" after death. After death, "in my flesh [personhood] shall I see God" (19:26, KJV). Being even more specific, Job insists that it will be he himself, not some wraith-like "stranger," who will see God (19:27). At least for the moment, Job is confident of surviving the crisis of impending death.

The book of Job reflects the changing mood of post-Exilic Hebrew thought about life after death. Indeed, its author may have been one of the influential forces of the change. Through most of the Old Testament Sheol is accepted as the destination of the dead. But in late pre-Christian Judaism there is seen a growing commitment to the hope for life after death. The book of Daniel is an example (see 12:2-3), as are Ecclesiasticus and

Wisdom of Solmon, two books of the Apocrypha, Jewish religious writings of the immediate pre-Christian era. In Jesus' day the issue of resurrection of the dead was a source of heated controversy between the two leading religious groups in Judaism. The Sadducees, contending that the doctrine was inconsistent with the main teaching of their Scripture, denied it. The Pharisees, holding that God's revelation was not limited to the earlier writings, affirmed the resurrection of the dead.

It may surprise us that our spiritual forebears waited until nearly the time of Christ's coming to consider seriously the belief in resurrection, but it should not. Others around them had elaborate rituals celebrating the afterlife, and it was the pagan nature of these rituals which doubtless turned the Hebrew mind, with its concept of a holy God, against the idea. A great many of these religious celebrations of life after death were associated with fertility and annual rebirth of the earth. Egypt, Phoenicia, Babylonia, and Greece all fostered the belief that immortality was achieved through communion with the fertility god. In Egypt it was the worship of Osiris. In Phoenicia, Israel's next-door neighbor, the worship of Adonis, god of fertility, and Astarte (Aphrodite), goddess of love, was promoted through sacred prostitution and sexual license believed to influence the productivity of the earth. Little wonder the prophet Elijah contended so fiercely with the priests of this religion of the Baal, and with Jezebel, Phoenician wife of Israel's King Ahab, and sponsor of Baalism in Israel (1 Kings 18:20-40).

In Babylonia the doctrine of the after life was built around one called Tammuz, who dies and rises again, being sought by Ishtar, the goddess of love and fertility. In Greece the belief in immortality arose from the Eleusinian and Dionysian mystery cults, which were essentially sexually-oriented and related to the fertility of the earth. Wherever one looked in the ancient world, except in Israel, elaborate rituals relating to the afterlife and usually associated with fertility, could be found. Israel, believing in a holy God and in a covenant relationship with him as his peculiar people, thought not so much of the individual's destiny as of the confidence of her perpetuity as Yahweh's chosen people on the earth.

Our Lord came into the midst of the speculation and controversy about the resurrection and confidently announced it. Moreover, for us Christians he forever settled the matter by his own resurrection. We believe in the resurrection, not out of some sentimental wish or because we have been convinced by the logic of such a claim. We believe because Christ was raised from the dead. And because he lives, we shall live also.

It is a sober moment when a man realizes that he has but one life on this earth and he begins to wonder whether or not that one life has permanent meaning. During his lifetime some three billion other human beings will be born, live, and die. And if he dares to reflect upon the fact that this life process has been going on generation after generation and century after century, for God only knows how long, it puts in a new light the one life he has to live.

Job understood the issue. Do we? Or do we, like some, refuse to think about it? Shall we try to evade by saturating consciousness with sensate experience so that the inner voice raising the question is drowned out by the noise? Shall we play the pathetic game of piling up goods, or fame, indulging ourselves in the futile fancy that we shall be remembered by those who come after us? Or shall we dispense with the problem with an airy wave of the hand and the "brave" conclusion that life is without meaning, that history is a pointless parade, processing from nowhere and recessing to the same destination? Christians have no cause or right to elect any of those ways of dealing with the issue of life and death, for the resurrection of Christ has given us both a hope and a responsibility.

In the Nuremburg war-crime trials, so the late Paul Tillich wrote in a sermon, a witness appeared who had lived for a time in a grave in a Jewish cemetery in Wilna, Poland. It was the only place he and many others could hide to escape the gas chamber. During this time he wrote poetry, and one of the poems was a description of a birth. In a grave nearby a young woman gave birth to a baby boy. The eighty-year-old grave-digger, wrapped in a shroud, assisted. When the newborn child uttered his first cry the old man prayed: "Great God, hast Thou finally sent the Messiah to us? For who else than the Messiah himself can be born in a grave?"[1] But after three days the poet saw the child sucking his mother's tears because she had no milk for him.

This story, which—as Dr. Tillich pointed out—surpasses anything the human imagination could invent, reminds us that the victory we Christians celebrate was won in a grave. Perhaps the overwhelming greatness of the resurrection has been lost to us because we have taken it too much for granted. We have forgotten that our Lord's friends did not return from Golgotha with joy and expectancy. We have forgotten that they felt it was the end, that he had been defeated, and that his death closed an era in their lives which had been deliriously glorious. We have lost the exhiliration that came with his resurrection because we have lost any sense of the finality of his death.

The old Jewish gravedigger knew better. He knew that life may not be expected to come from a grave. "But," as Paul put it, "the truth is, Christ was raised to life—the firstfruits of the harvest of the dead" (1 Cor. 15:20, NEB). And because this new life was "born in a grave" we can answer the question of the song, "Is that all there is?" with a resounding no, for "eye hath not seen, nor ear heard, neither have entered into the heart of man, the things which God hath prepared for them that love him" (1 Cor. 2:9, KJV).

Conclusion: "My Redeemer Lives"

The book of Job is a profound testimony to God and man. God is sovereign Lord, deserving man's adoration and obedience. Man is endowed with dignity and worth, though he may be pilloried by terrifying circumstance. He is also insufficient and, despite his courage and pride, is unable to save himself, requiring God's grace. Job is a prelude to the gospel, but it is not the gospel. It cites man's need and hails God's adequacy. We look at Job's suffering and are appalled, but the note of God's suffering on Job's account is missing. There is little show of divine tenderness. No "almighty sob" is heard from the whirlwind. No sign of the cross is displayed. God proclaims his "Godness"; Job repents of his presumptiousness, and in the end he is restored.

In our view, Archibald MacLeish has misinterpreted Job by overstating the case of divine lovelessness in Job, but it is not hard to see how it could happen. In his play, *J. B.,* the hero says of God at the end of the play, "He does not love. He Is." MacLeish missed the devout theism of the book of Job, turning his play into a plea for humanism. J. B.'s wife, replying to his claim that God does not love, says: "But we do. That's the wonder."' J. B.'s God is a mindless, careless irresistible force. That is not Job's God, the one who comes to rebuke Job for presuming that God was in his debt because he had lived uprightly. But neither is Job's view of God Hosea's.

Why should it be? it may be asked. Precisely. It need not, to be authentic. Job's message concerning God is of divine sovereignty. Hosea's is of divine mercy and tenderness, as Amos' is of divine righteousness. Only those who demand that every page of the Bible tell the whole story of redemption will be troubled at the thought that the book of Job is an incomplete revelation. The writer of the letter to the Hebrews was under no such illusion. He began by making it clear that only in Christ do we see the fulness of God. "When in former times God spoke to our forefathers, he spoke in fragmentary and varied fashion through the prophets. But in this the final age he has spoken to us in the Son" (Heb. 1:1-2, NEB). Everything before him is fragmentary; in the Son, God "put it all together."

Job does not stand at the end of the full revelation. He sees it from afar, and his heart leaps up in hope that the awful separation which he feels between deity and humanity will be done away. He knows that he cannot cross the chasm from his finiteness to God's infiniteness. Through suffering he learns that he cannot be his own bridge-builder. Might there be One who would conduct him safely over the abyss that separates him from the Almighty, and who might stand beside him in his helplessness?

In at least three places in the book, Job envisions that "noble other"—not an earthly friend, with all of the human frailties Job himself suffers from—who will stand up for him and defend him in his weakness. The first is spoken in a defiant mood, Job being confident of his innocence and wanting only the opportunity to present his case to God without fear of further affliction. But he is overmatched, he says, and "There is no umpire between us, who might lay his hand upon us both" (9.33). Who is this "Mediator" needed to stand between man and God? Is it not he who, in the words of Paul, "is at the right hand of God, who indeed intercedes for us?" (Rom. 8:34). Job's motive for wanting to come before God may not have been the best, but his understanding of his need of someone to be for him a "Bridge Over Troubled Waters" sounds the authentic note.

The second shaft of heavenly light on the problem of man's need for divine assistance to transcend his human situation shines in Job 16:18-19. Job appears at this point to have given up any hope of earthly vindication, so he must look to the next world. He cries out that his case not be "covered up" and simply forgotten. But the hope that he has for eventual justice is in heaven:

"Even now, behold, my witness is in heaven, and he that vouches for me is on high" (16:19). The umpire-mediator has now become a witness. He will not only seek to obtain a fair trial for Job, but will testify on his behalf.

The third allusion brings Job even closer to the gospel. It is the beautiful affirmation of Job 19:25: "For I know that my Redeemer lives, and at last he will stand upon the earth." He is not only mediator and witness. Job, who began by claiming an innocence needing only an impartial hearing to be verified, no longer seeks acquittal, but redemption. He requires more than an umpire and a witness. He needs a Savior. We all do.

The message of the gospel is that we *have* One. In Christ I find my Mediator—not one more tender and loving than God, but God reaching out to my humanity. In Christ I find my Witness—not one there to defend me before an angry judge eager for an opportunity to "throw the book at me," but one who is God-become-man and who knows my human predicament, counting me worth saving just the same. In Christ I find my Redeemer—not one who is different from God but who is God acting in love toward me to save me in my estrangement from him and from my brothers.

NOTES

Chapter 1

1. Marvin H. Pope, *Job*, "The Anchor Bible" (Garden City, N. Y.: Doubleday & Co., Inc., 1965), p. xxx.

2. For a concise and reliable summary of the evidence on this matter see S. R. Driver and G. B. Gray, *The Book of Job*, "International Critical Commentary" (Edinburgh: T. T. Clark, 1921), pp. xxxi-xxxiv.

3. Andrew Bruce Davidson, *The Book of Job*, "The Cambridge Bible" (Cambridge: Cambridge University Press, 1889); H. Wheeler Robinson, *The Cross in the Old Testament* (Philadelphia: Westminster Press, 1955); Samuel Terrien, *Job: Poet of Existence* (New York: Bobbs-Merrill Co., Inc., 1957); Edward J. Kissane, *The Book of Job* (Dublin: Browne & Nolan, Ltd., 1939); Robert Gordis, *The Book of God and Man* (Chicago: University of Chicago Press, 1965).

Chapter 2

1. William Barclay, *The Gospel of Matthew*, "The Daily Bible Study Series" (Philadelphia: Westminster Press, 1956), p. 178.

Chapter 9

1. Boston: Houghton Mifflin Co., 1958, p. 11.

2. *Ibid.*, pp. 12-13.

3. Albert Schweitzer, *On the Edge of the Primeval Forest* (London: A. & C. Black, Ltd., 1948), p. 116.

4. Thornton Wilder, *The Angel That Troubles the Water* (New York: Coward-McCann, 1928), pp. 147-49.

Chapter 11

1. Paul Tillich, *The Shaking of the Foundations* (New York: Charles Scribner's Sons, 1948), p. 165.

Conclusion

1. MacLeish, p. 152.